THE
CREATED
RELATIONSHIP

How to create successful
relationships with anyone.

DEE STEVENS

BALBOA.
PRESS
A DIVISION OF HAY HOUSE

Balboa Press books may be ordered through booksellers or by contacting:

Balboa Press
A Division of Hay House
1663 Liberty Drive
Bloomington, IN 47403
www.balboapress.com
1 (877) 407-4847

Because of the dynamic nature of the Internet, any web addresses or links contained in this book may have changed since publication and may no longer be valid. The views expressed in this work are solely those of the author and do not necessarily reflect the views of the publisher, and the publisher hereby disclaims any responsibility for them.

The author of this book does not dispense medical advice or prescribe the use of any technique as a form of treatment for physical, emotional, or medical problems without the advice of a physician, either directly or indirectly. The intent of the author is only to offer information of a general nature to help you in your quest for emotional and spiritual well-being. In the event you use any of the information in this book for yourself, which is your constitutional right, the author and the publisher assume no responsibility for your actions.

Any people depicted in stock imagery provided by Thinkstock are models, and such images are being used for illustrative purposes only.
Certain stock imagery © Thinkstock.

Print information available on the last page.

ISBN: 978-1-5043-6546-8 (sc)
ISBN: 978-1-5043-6547-5 (hc)
ISBN: 978-1-5043-6571-0 (e)

Library of Congress Control Number: 2016914451

Balboa Press rev. date: 09/13/2016

Contents

Acknowledgements

I am grateful to my partner, lover, and best friend David Rutter, who not only believed that I could do it but gave me the space and support to write this book. He allowed me to use our stories, and he also read the book cover to cover twice and gave me his feedback. Without this support, I might have always dreamed of writing a book but never acted on it.

For many of the ideas and the constant push forward to accomplish my dreams, I thank Landmark Worldwide Education. The programs that I took in the last twelve years have supported me every step of the way in building my confidence and opening my world up to what I could accomplish.

I thank my family, both my parents and my daughters, for the relationship experience they have provided me and lessons that it has taught over the years.

I thank the relationship authors that have gone before me that not only have shown me what I need to know to improve my own relationships but have also inspired many of my creative ideas for this book. These authors are John Gray, Iyanla Vanzant, M. Scott Peck MD, Neale Donald Walsch, Gary Chapman, Dr. Barbara De Angelis, Harriet Lerner Ph.D., and others.

Preface

I thought long and hard about what gives me the authority to write a relationship book. What makes me believe that I can give advice about relationships? I am not a psychologist or a therapist. I have not spent years in school learning the psychology around human behavior and how people came to where they are now. I am a lover of love. From the time when I first read Disney books about young girls finding their true loves and living happily ever after, I have sought out whatever I can find about love, how to find it, how to receive it, and how to give it unconditionally. I have read book after book by many authors that I adore on the subject. I have gone to many workshops on the subject and discovered what some of the experts have said about it. I have plain lived it myself.

Many of the procedures and much of the advice that I have included in this book are things that I discovered by reading or trying instructions that I have learned. I have not had the most model relationships. I have had major heartbreaks in my life. I have had daughters that have hated me at times and coworkers that I couldn't be around; however, through most of these experiences, I have learned plenty about what it takes to be in relationships and to make them work. I am not one to let relationships be what they will be. I have learned over the years that either you must take responsibility for them and create what you want in your relationships or else you become a victim, and your life and relationships become one tragedy after another.

This book is filled with my own personal stories and outlines the strategy that I have discovered along the way that has gotten me through life. These stories have made me who

I am today, and I know that I am not at the end of my learning about relationships. I continue to see relationships that I need to tend to. When I find myself resenting or judging the people around me, that is my wake-up call that I need to work on another relationship.

Introduction

As I have found the right teachers, authors, and mentors that have taught me what it is to love and be loved, you have found yourself reading this book, and you are in for new revelations and breakthroughs to occur for you. To begin with, you need to look at the relationships in your life and where they could use improvement. Maybe there are some that you have written off and no longer want in your life. Unfortunately, the hole that is left where they used to be can be a reminder that you are not complete. Maybe you don't have that many relationships in your life, and you would like to develop more. Perhaps you have relationships all around you that are not as satisfying as you would like, and you want to know how to make them deeper and more intimate. Maybe you are on the verge of a divorce, and this is the last idea you have had to make it work. Whatever brought you here, you have found the right book. This book will be a resource for improving any relationship, whether it is with family members, coworkers, business partners, lovers, or yourself. Let my journey of heartbreak, depression, rejection, self-actualization, love, and romance inspire you and lead you on your own journey where you become the author, take control of what happens in your relationships, and never leave them to chance anymore.

In this book, you will find advice not only on how to improve your current relationships but also on how to create them from the ground up. You will find that you have more control over your relationships than you ever imagined possible, and all you need to do is take the reins and create them.

It is recommended that you keep a journal available while you read this book for some of the exercises that are suggested. This will allow you to have a greater insight into how you already operate and to try some new strategies for your relationships.

Responsibility in Created Relationships

Most people think that the word *responsibility* means there is blame or guilt involved. Here is the definition of responsibility according to *Merriam-Webster*:

Responsibility

: the state of being or the person who caused something to happen
: a duty or task that you are required or expected to do
: something that you should do because it is morally right, legally required, etc.

Here's the bad news: responsibility is seeing that you caused your relationships to be the way they are. The exciting news is that you have the ability to cause them to be any way that you would like them to be.

You might be thinking, "But wait a minute! I didn't cause my husband to cheat on me." And you would be right there. You don't have the power to control how another person behaves in a relationship. You do, however, have the power to create how you respond to the people in your life, regardless of their behavior.

Let's say that your husband does cheat on you. That makes him the bad guy in the marriage. But let's say that when you find out he cheated on you, you rip his clothes into little shreds and throw them out the window, screaming at the top of your lungs names that I would not repeat. The neighbors all look your way to see what is going on. You become the raging lunatic that the police take away, and he is able to go to the department store with your joint account and have his new babe pick out his new wardrobe.

Many people argue that they didn't have any other choice except to respond the way they did. I have heard it many times from my students: "He hit me, so I hit him."

"What else could you have done?" I ask.

"Nothing! He made me angry."

This goes to show that people are letting their emotions run their responses in life instead of having real "response ability" that can turn things around and give them the power to make rational decisions that are not burning bridges with people they love.

Living in Victimville

Unfortunately, most of us live in a world that I call Victimville, where it is natural to put the responsibility, or actually blame, on someone or something else. If you are late to work, it is the traffic's fault. If your report is late, it was the computer's fault. If you are mean to the people you love, it's because they were in the wrong first and you were only reacting.

You can't help coming up with excuses for your failures because you were indoctrinated in this as a child. You might have watched your parents blame each other and begun to blame your siblings or your friends for your mistakes. You watched your friends use excuses with their parents, and you learned that this is purely how life is, one excuse after another.

It became a way to avoid pain, and now you do it as a defense mechanism. The thought of taking responsibility for your failures can give you anxiety and angst—so much so that you begin to make up little lies to cover your faults and convince yourself that they are true. The lies you tell yourself become real in your mind, and you will defend them to no end. You even expect lies from others and don't like it if they don't have acceptable excuses.

You might think your white lies will keep you out of trouble with other people, but instead, they put walls up between you and them. People that you blame begin to resent and not trust you. The person that you give excuses to time after time starts to see you as small and not in control of your life. It causes people not to trust you to follow through with the tasks they need you to do. These stories of why your life is not working and how others are causing this become ingrained patterns that continue to surface over and over again, and you are helpless to take any action because it is all somebody else's fault.

One pattern that I faced was I used to go from job to job. In these jobs, I encountered women bosses that, in my opinion, didn't appreciate how hard I worked, or the amount of time I was taking to do a job. It started with my manager at the pizza place I worked at as a teen. She would sometimes bring me to her office and yell at me till I cried. I was solely a young teenager at the time and thought all bosses did this (after all, my dad's bosses yelled at him). I didn't like it; on the other hand, I thought that bosses needed to be tough to manage people.

No matter what I did at this job, my boss would not see me as capable. She would have me train person after person, and she would promote some of my trainees instead of me. Finally after four years, I one day asked her why she would not make me an assistant manager.

She looked at me as if I was crazy for asking that question and answered, "You are simply not management material." She said it so matter-of-factly that I began to believe that I would always work for someone else and never be promoted.

One day she brought me into her office to discuss my less than white shirt (why we wore white in a pizza restaurant was beyond me).

"Your shirt is looking gray, when are you going to replace it?" she asked in a stern tone.

"I'm not," I answered defiantly feeling powerful to be standing up to her for once.

"Why not?" she asked.

"Because I'm looking for a new job," I answered lying, but with every intention to begin looking.

"You have two weeks to find another job!" she began yelling.

"No, I will leave now!" I retorted, handed her my badge and then walked out.

When I left, I was proud of myself for not breaking down and crying in front of her like I had so many times. This was her fault, and she would have to do without me.

I would later see this pattern again in a job I took years later. I was teaching and had a principal who was once again a powerful woman. I felt that I worked hard at this job, even though I had difficult students with emotional disabilities. At the end of the year, she let me go without ever having given me an evaluation or letting me know what I was doing wrong. I thought I could fight this with the union because she wasn't giving me a chance. When I found out that probationary teachers didn't have to have an evaluation or even a reason to be let go, I left without asking why. Once again, it was her fault, and she had always wanted me to fail from the beginning.

One day I was at my third job, where I had a powerful woman boss. I loved this post and wanted to one day retire from there. I got that familiar call to the office that made my stomach tighten and head pound. I once again sat in front of another woman with tears in my eyes as she said to me, "You don't have the leadership capabilities that we need in this position."

These were almost exactly the same words I had heard from my pizza place manager. It took me straight back to that time in my life where I was unable to please my boss. I had enough sense and introspection to recognize the pattern that I was in. I began to see that it was not my boss's fault that I was showing up weak. It was mine. Maybe I needed to look at myself. I then saw that the reason administrators didn't see my value was because I was avoiding them. Ever since my first job in a pizza joint, I avoided being around people in authority. I avoided seeking out their help. I avoided talking to them casually. At meetings, I avoided sitting in their vicinity and stayed silent the whole time. I had thought hiding from them was the answer. It wasn't.

I bravely set up a meeting with my assistant principal. I was shaking as I entered her office, but I was determined to let her know what I had discovered about myself. I could tell that she was not sure of what I was going to say to her and didn't know if I was still angry or sad. I sat down in the padded chairs, still shaking and I said, "The reason that I wanted to talk to you was that I haven't allowed you to get to know me."

"How so?" she asked.

"I have been hiding from you all my faults and mistakes and not letting you help me with them."

"Like what?" she asked.

"Like I'm unorganized and have a difficult time finding the materials I need when I'm teaching. I'm also scared of you, and when you are in the room watching me, I get nervous, and it looks as though I don't know what I'm doing. This shows up like I am weak and I understand that. I'm not weak with the students when you are not around," I said beginning to gain my power back as I revealed my secrets to her.

"Why do I make you nervous?" she inquired.

"I believe it started with my mother or even my first boss, but whenever I am faced with a powerful woman, I hide. I even blame the woman for making me weak, but I see now that it is my own fault."

This conversation went on for some time afterward and with each secret that I revealed to her, I became more confident. We talked on for a long time past the fifteen minutes that I requested. It was like we were old friends. She wished me well and hugged me. I left her office determined that I would no longer hide from my bosses.

Whenever we live in Victimville, we end up giving our power and our happiness away to the other person or organization. We love to blame our government for the evils that we claim they are doing to us. How many of us are willing to propose a new idea, or voice our opinion? Many people believe that the world is out to get them, and they are not safe. They put themselves into a prison of their own making. They hate anyone, and everyone for what they perceive is being done to them. This is not the way that most people would choose to live. Nevertheless, they choose it anyway.

When you finally understand that you created your life and your relationships, you can then become free. You begin to see the power in yourself and believe that you can create whatever you put your mind to. You let yourself out of the prison and start to live life intentionally. That is the beginning of responsibility.

> When you think everything is someone else's
> fault, you will suffer a lot. When you realize that
> everything springs only from yourself, you will learn
> both peace and joy.
> —The Dalai Lama

Journal activity: Where in your life are you a victim? Who are the people in your life that you feel are holding you back or abusing you in some way?

Taking Responsibility

We have heard that relationships should be fifty-fifty. Actually, they should be 100 percent you and 0 percent the other person. You can't control the other side. You might be saying to yourself that you don't know if you are in the right relationship or whether it is worth putting in the effort. More than likely, because you are creating this relationship, you are going to create the next one in the same way that you have created this one. You might as well go to work on the one that you have in front of you now and see where it can go.

Taking responsibility in a relationship can be refreshing. It can show people how vulnerable you can be and how willing you are to make a relationship work. It builds trust.

Going back to my job situations, I finally found a job that I created. I had envisioned a situation where people saw what I did and appreciated me for the work I put in. Instead of ducking the bosses, I went to any event that the principals were at. I even stepped out of my comfort zone and went on a hike up a Fourteener with my new administrators. When I was late with my paperwork, I did not make excuses. I apologized for the lateness and set a new deadline. I would then ensure that I had it in, no matter how much work I had to take home to do it. Most of the time, my paperwork was not late, and I was candid if I saw a problem arising that would make it late. I was no longer going to hide my issues in the dark. My administrators, in my first year, saw my integrity and decided to let me have the staffing chair responsibilities the following year.

Taking responsibility allows you to create what you want in life. I often see it as the magic that draws to you the tools you need to be successful. When you are no longer a victim, you are free to create. It takes the belief that you can create whatever you envision.

Breaking free from the victim mentality is not as easy as we would like it to be. We are accustomed to it and surround ourselves with others who are just as accustomed to it. We might know people who, when you give them answers to problems, come back with a reason about how that won't work, because they don't believe they can affect the outcomes of their lives and instead live in the world of victimhood.

So how do you break away from that victim mentality and take on being responsible? How do you trust that if you do assume responsibility for your mistakes, someone won't benefit from the chance to prove how incompetent you are? You have to have faith to try it. You can begin by looking into how you deal with the problems in your life.

Problems

Buddha taught that life is suffering. Face it—we can't have lives without having problems once in a while. In fact, those of us who have the highest aspirations also have the biggest problems. When Gandhi once said that he wanted the British to leave India, he faced some colossal problems. He lived his life attacking his problems, unlike many of us, who live our lives avoiding obstacles that come our way. We create distractions from our issues and sometimes numb our struggles with food, alcohol, or other addictions. Many people think if they ignore a situation enough, it will go away on its own, and unfortunately, that is not true. The problems get worse.

The good news is that as you handle your problems within your relationships, you build your character. You begin to see yourself as someone who handles problems with ease. You will find yourself getting closer to people in your life because you are not avoiding talking about the elephant in the room.

The first step in solving problems is believing that you can solve most problems as long as you take the time to do it. Some of us might have limiting thoughts about ourselves because of past experiences and don't believe that we are capable of solving problems. I was one of those people when it came to mechanical gadgets. My dad could fix about any machinery you put in front of him, and I married a man who was similar to him. I didn't have to know anything about machines in my life until one night when the pilot light on the furnace went out in my mobile home. I was terrified that if I didn't light the furnace, my pipes would freeze. I would then have a bigger problem that I was not financially ready to handle. My dad was living 250 miles away. He described how to do it over the phone, and I only half listened because I had a belief that I could not fix any machine.

The night became colder, and I put my three-year-old and newborn into my waterbed while I tried to figure out what to do. Eventually, I decided that I was going to do it and could do it. I started by intently looking at the furnace and reading some of the instructions on it. I played with some knobs, and I tried lighting it a couple of times and failed. I thought many times about giving up and blaming my ex if my pipes froze. Once again, I had to tell myself that I could do this. Nowadays, I simply Google videos on subjects and watch them till I know what to do; however, back then, we didn't have that kind of technology. Finally, I took the time to analyze what I had done and not done, read the instructions some more, and thought about how the furnace probably worked. I then turned the right knob while pushing in and lit the pilot light all on my own. It was the first of many actions that I took on my own that began to build my confidence in myself as a single mother.

To be able to light that pilot light, I had to admit that it was my problem and that it was up to me to solve it. Many times in our relationships, we don't see the distance between us and others as our problem to solve. We might be waiting for an apology from someone else and feel that the problem is all on the other person's shoulders. We continue to avoid those people, and the disputes get worse. We don't see that we also have the responsibility to call them and begin rebuilding the relationships that used to hold meaning.

Growing up, my brother and I were very close. We would sneak into each other's rooms and share stories until our parents overheard us or until we got tired and went to our own rooms. We would tell each other about our relationships and our friends. We shared a lot of the same friends and hung out together after I left home. After I had got married, we saw each other less, and after he had got married, we began to talk only at holidays. I blamed my sister-in-law because I thought she didn't like our family and only wanted him to be part of her family. Later, when I saw this, I apologized to her for the thoughts that I'd been having. Still, my brother and I didn't seem to be close. Finally, I realized after my mother died and we had been spending more time around each other that we were still as close as we ever were; it was just that neither one of us was making the effort to get together. I then began calling him more often and setting up times to see him. I was the big sister, and he probably wondered why I had quit including him, and all the while I thought that he was not including me.

Journal activity: What are some problems that you have been avoiding or waiting for others to solve for you?

Choices

What takes you out of Victimville is the awareness that life provides a buffet of choices that you can make. Choices come with consequences, and we can't always predict those consequences. Still, the ability to choose is freeing. In relationships, we have many choices. We can choose to go slowly or choose to go fast. We can choose to marry or choose to stay single. We can choose to forgive or choose to be angry. We can choose to have sex right away or choose to wait. We can choose to have children or choose to not have children. Neale Walsch, author of *Conversations with God*, proclaims that every morning his wife and he choose whether to be married to each other that day or not.

These are the powerful choices that we can make that allow us to be the creators in life. Sometimes tragedies occur, and we end up feeling like victims again, helpless in the face of sickness, grief, or the inhumanity that someone can inflict on others. This can propel you straight into Victimville again. An example of this would be being raped; there is no doubt that you were a victim when you were raped because you didn't choose to have sex at the time. Even this scenario, you have choices, and discovering your choices makes you feel powerful over the situation instead of victimized. Your choices here are whether to report it to the authorities or not, whether to forgive or not, whether to blame yourself or blame the rapist, and whether to seek out help or not. There are many choices here as well, and you don't have to go through life as a victim, closing yourself off from future relationships. You don't want the rapist to continue to have victory over you and take more than he or she already has.

Two older men once raped me. They provided me hard alcohol when I was nineteen and then took turns with me as I was blacked out. After this, they took me to my car and let me drive home. I only remember bits and pieces of the night and what the two men did, and I don't remember the drive home at all. I chose to transfer jobs so I didn't have to see these men anymore, I chose to forgive them for what they did, and I chose to forgive myself for getting so drunk that I lost my ability to make appropriate choices. Yes, you read this right; I chose to forgive the men. Forgiving them didn't mean that what they did was right. I forgave them because doing so freed me from the shame of being a victim, and it allowed me to release my hatred and not carry it into my relationships in the future.

At the time of this incident, there were not many people being convicted of rape when the victim was too drunk to make choices, so I didn't think that I could report this to the police. Although I can't change the past, I can choose to teach my daughters and other young women about their choices as victims of rape. I chose not be a victim because of this incident any longer.

What stops most people from making choices is the fear that they will make the wrong ones. This could be a fear of failure and not achieving the results that you were hoping for. So what people do instead is go around avoiding choices that could really make a difference in their lives.

The risks in life that sometimes fail are what make us feel alive. Sometimes you overthink choices and make them more complicated than they have to be. You might not make choices because you are not sure what your instinct is telling you about the decisions. You might think that not making choices is the best option and that you are letting life take its course; however, not making a choice is a choice in itself and comes with consequences as well. The consequences are that you are not controlling your own destiny and writing your own story.

Overcoming your fear of choosing can be very powerful. If you have difficulty in this area, begin looking at many of the choices that you make on a daily basis. You managed to dress yourself this morning, chose food that got you through your day, and chose a route to work that got you there safely. Not all choices are significant, and you are making them on a regular basis. When looking at the more important choices in life, you can step outside yourself and imagine that you are a close friend giving the advice. You can ask for suggestions from others when you can't decide what to do. Eventually, you will learn that whatever choices you make, they are the right ones. You can learn to turn ones that don't have favorable outcomes into valuable lessons that you won't repeat in the future.

Journal activity: What are some choices in your life that you have avoided making and have regretted later? What are some choices that you have made that you are proud of? What are some choices you have made that you are not so proud of, but that you learned some good lessons from? What are some choices that you can make right now that you have been avoiding?

Choosing Versus Reacting

Most of us want to have response-ability, which is the ability to control how we react to situations. We want to be able to say whatever we want to say at the moment and not say something that we will regret later. What stops us from having this ability is our emotions, usually fear, hurt, and anger. Anger often stems from pain or fear and is a secondary emotion. To be able to choose what we are going to say or do at any moment takes a lot of stepping away from our emotions and choosing what is best to do at the moment.

I have found that what helps my ability to respond in the ways that I want to respond is to be curious about how certain events trigger my feelings. I have developed a curiosity about why it is that I am having an emotional reaction to what another person is saying or doing around me. A trigger usually stems from some event in the past that is affecting us right now in the present and has little to do with the person or situation that we are dealing with.

As a teacher, I have had a lot of practice with this. I work in middle school, and middle schoolers can be very cruel at times. They know what to say to get under each other's skin and can do this with their teachers. Students are notorious for seeing flaws in a person's clothing. They will notice a stain, a tear or something that doesn't fit well and it becomes the object of their entertainment. The minute that I hear snickering, I begin checking myself over to see what they are seeing. I would either shut down or become angry after awhile but was unable to have the response-ability that I wanted. Eventually, I saw that it was not the students that I had in front of me that were causing my frustration, but that they were triggering events from my past.

When I was in junior high, a large girl bullied me. She was so mean that even the boys were afraid of her. She had lots of influence in my school, and pretty soon, more people were bullying me. I had hand-me-down clothing from my cousin, and my clothes rarely fit properly. My clothing was not the latest style, nor clothing that I looked right in. I hated my clothes, and kids at school could sense this and pointed out the flaws they saw in my clothing. I can still hear the kids harassing me about my too-short pants: "Are you waiting for a flood?" I pulled away or cried, and it only made matters worse because they knew they had gotten to me.

Eventually, I saw that some middle schoolers will do whatever it takes to gain power over their teachers. I started to have more curiosity about the students that did this. I wondered about their home lives and whether they were growing up someplace where they felt powerless or were being bullied. I began to not react. I was able to laugh at myself and give comebacks like, "What? This isn't the latest style? They lied to me at the thrift store where I bought it." When the students realized that they couldn't get under my skin, they no longer tried to bully me. When my daughters struggled with bullies, I taught them how to respond to bullies in a way that would defuse the situation. Too bad I didn't have these skills back in junior high school with my bully.

You might have people in your life that you metaphorically dance with that know how to step on your toes and make you fall to the floor whenever they have the chance. They might be deriving some power out of this reaction, or revenge of some kind. You end up responding in a way that is vengeful, and the dance goes on. Now is the time to look at this response and ask yourself why you are so hurt, fearful, or angry about what these people are doing. Look to see where the patterns lie. Have they done this before? Have others, such as your parents, done this? Many of our problems we experience in relationships mirror problems we had with our parents.

Choose not to have this response ever again. If you are someone who allows people to get under your skin, and you end up retaliating in violent or brutal ways, choose to walk away until you have had a deeper look at why you are so inflamed by what these people said or did. Let them know that you will avoid this kind of reaction in the future. Make sure you keep your word about that. If you don't know why they are choosing to push buttons they know will hurt you, there is nothing like an inquiry to turn the tables on people who are on the attack.

I have come right out and asked students, "Why do you want to talk about my clothes during our lesson? Are you trying to distract me?" I do it matter-of-factly, with no charge in my voice, and it usually stops the student right away. If you can't ask a question without emotion or charge, don't do it, because you will receive more argument.

Experts will tell you to take deep breaths, count to ten, or excuse yourself so you can pull yourself together and be able to respond without blowing up. I find that being curious about my anger or the other person's anger usually works far better for me because I discover what my anger is trying to tell me, and through that, I begin to know myself better and recognize when it happens again. In fact, I like to use my emotion to grow in my life. Whenever I have an emotional response to a circumstance, I don't blame the other person for my response. I take on the responsibility to acknowledge that the problem is mine and that I need to seek out the root of it and why it bothers me.

Journal activity: What are some circumstances that are frustrating you and making you react in ways that you are not proud of? What events from your past remind you of what is happening now? What questions do you have about the people who seem to push your buttons? What questions could you ask them when they say what they do?

Not Taking Responsibility

Some people blame themselves for whatever happens, and that is not what taking responsibility means. Some people take on other people's problems and see themselves as the heroes who have to solve these problems. We as parents do this frequently in our relationships with our children. We sometimes don't see our kids as separate from ourselves, with an independent right to choose as well. If our children get into trouble or become addicted to drugs, we feel that it is our fault and that we somehow forced them to live this life. They can blame us for infractions that they perceive we did or didn't do. If we don't give kids material items, they said we didn't love them and denied them the gadgets that other parents gave their children; if we give them whatever they want, they blame us for spoiling them. Let's face it: there is no perfect way to raise a child. When we allow ourselves to be sucked into taking responsibility for many of our children's faults, we are not being productive as parents. I find that the beginning of the Serenity Prayer is my go-to when I find myself overwhelmed and trying to fix a problem that is not my own.

> God, grant me the serenity
> to accept the things I cannot change,
> courage to change the things I can,
> and wisdom to know the difference.

So how do you know when you are trying to solve a problem that is not your own? You know this when it requires influencing, fixing, or doing more for a person than that person is doing for him- or herself. Trying to take responsibility for other people's problems can be frustrating because you don't have the ability to make them do or think what you want them to, no matter how you try and how often you argue. People grow stronger and more resilient after solving their own problems. That is true love.

I have been guilty of this myself with my daughters. I let them live with me without acquiring a job and doing things for themselves. I avoided kicking them out of my home because that is what my mother did to me at the age of eighteen, and I knew it had been hard for me to get on my feet and take care of myself. I knew that I had struggled, and I didn't want my daughters to have that kind of pain. Eventually, after my daughter got pregnant at twenty, I knew that I had not prepared her to be a mother. I did finally kick her out and expect her to find her own way. I still help her when I can, and when I can't or don't want to, I honestly tell her how strong she is and how capable she is of solving her own problems. I let her know that I believe in her and am proud of what she has accomplished so far. I acknowledge her frequently for how brave she is to be a young single mother and how capable she is with her son. I'm not fixing her or her problems. I'm empowering her to do this on her own. She respects and appreciates me far more now than when she was living with me and I was meeting most of her needs.

Journal activity: Look into your life and see where you are taking responsibility for people and problems that are not yours. Are you allowing others to blame you for some problem that they believe is your fault? What does it cost you to continue to take on this responsibility, either financially or emotionally? Where are you enabling or crippling others, preventing them from growing? What conversations can you see yourself having with them that would empower them to take on their own problems?

Created Integrity

The definition of integrity according to *Merriam-Webster* is this:

Integrity

: the quality of being honest and fair

: the state of being complete or whole

Honest and Fair

Honesty

Often we are not completely honest in our relationships. We lie, or we withhold the whole truth to avoid the pain that comes with telling the truth. President Clinton withheld the whole truth about Monica Lewinsky and his indiscretions with her to avoid facing the media and his wife with the truth about what happened. He claimed in front of the whole world, "I did not have sexual relations with that woman." As many of us know, he hid that he had received oral sex from her.

This is like a four-year-old who is racing around the house, breaks a lamp, and then says, "It fell and broke." He doesn't see that his actions were what caused the lamp to break because he didn't do it on purpose. Many adults have that four-year-old inside them driving their normal lives, and they rarely have the experience of having mature, adult relationships based on honesty and trust.

You might have some secret that you are hiding and justify it with, "I'm trying to protect him from the truth because he couldn't handle it."

That might be what you are saying to yourself; however, you need to look deeply into the question of whether you are in actuality protecting him or yourself. If he has suspicions about you, this is frustrating for him because he senses that the relationship is a charade, although he can't explain why. This can make him imagine many situations, including ones that are worse than what actually happened. You might be hiding that a coworker has a crush on you because you don't plan on ever acting on it. Because you are keeping it from your partner, he might imagine that you are actually having an affair or having thoughts about an affair. If you are completely honest, he learns to trust you.

It's not easy to be completely honest in a relationship. We are insecure beings, and we feel that if we are vulnerable with people, they will take advantage of this vulnerability or use the things we tell them as weapons against us later. They might not trust us wholeheartedly because they see our mistakes. If we want to create real relationships that are deep and meaningful and not merely surface, we need to be able to be vulnerable with people. We have to trust that if they use it against us, leave us, or begin to see our flaws, we are able to handle it.

I had a relationship with a man who valued his privacy, which to me meant he had to be hiding some secret from me. I thought it was strange that he would grow close and then push me away. I felt I was justified in investigating what he was up to. I had come out of a relationship where I was cheated on for most of the time it lasted. I had felt like a fool for not being more aware of what was going on. So I decided I was going to spy on him, and whatever I found, I was not going to confront him on it. I went through his backpack while he was in the shower. I felt very deceitful doing it. I found a letter to him that I suspected was from another woman. I was afraid to open it because although I wanted answers, there was a part of me that was afraid of the answers as well. The letter was not from a woman, and I was ashamed of myself for reading it—so ashamed that I know he sensed that I was hiding information from him. We broke up. Many years later when I spoke with him, I did tell him about it. It was not easy, but I had had many more lessons in integrity by then, and I knew that it was the right action to take. He was upset, and he said that there was some reason he felt he could not trust me, and this could have been it.

Many times, opening up about deep, dark secrets can be a release as well and get them off your chest. I heard on the radio a woman who had gotten pregnant with a man's baby and aborted the baby without telling him because the relationship was not working. She later got back together with him, and they were engaged to be married. She struggled with the decision of whether to tell him or to continue to keep the secret. Many of the callers that called to give her advice let her know that it was better to tell him now than to keep it secret and have it later come out in front of a doctor or somewhere else. My thought was that she had this dark secret that she was keeping and grieving over on her own. Telling him might be difficult at first; however, it could lead to a deeper relationship between the two of them. Her fiancé would have a better understanding of many of her emotions when it came to children and could support her through this. She had to trust that if he were going to reject her because of this, it would be better before the "I dos."

I have had many of these conversations with people I love, and they were not comfortable or easy. They were, however, necessary. For the difficult conversations that scared me to my very core, I learned that the following steps were helpful.

1. Make the decision that you are going to have this conversation no matter the results. It's like ripping a Band-Aid off and letting whatever consequences happen.
2. Decide on a time and place to have the conversation and ask the person to meet with you. This starts the motion in place, and you are impelled to finish it.
3. Write out in a letter what you are going to say.
4. Read the letter to a trusted friend to see if this is really what you want to say. Have the trusted friend or a coach hold you accountable to following through with the tough conversation. They can even wait by the phone in case you

19

need more support, or the conversation had consequences you were not expecting.

5. Remind yourself that if you mess up this conversation, you can always have another conversation and another until matters get complete.
6. Have the conversation or read them the letter.
7. Pay attention to their reactions. If they are defensive, then you didn't emphasize your own responsibility in the matter enough.
8. Thank them for letting you have this conversation.

Journal activity: What are some conversations that you have avoided having? What could become available to you if you have those conversations? What could this provide the other person that could make that person's life better? Write the other person a letter and see if you can be really honest in your letter. Who are some people you could get to support you as you approach this conversation?

Brutally Honest

Some people feel they are completely honest and don't mind telling others the flaws that they see in them. These people are unaware that what they say are hurting the other people more than clearing the air. If you pride yourself on telling people that their clothes are trashy and make them look like a tramp, or that they are becoming fat, or the many other critical words people say to others that are brutally honest, you are not creating relationships that have integrity.

Instead of being honest, you might be leveling people. When you are giving people negative messages that hurt them, you are probably trying to bring them down to a level where you feel superior to them to make yourself feel better. Being honest with integrity should be uncomfortable for you, and if it isn't, you need to ask yourself what kinds of subjects you are honest about. If it is much of the time about the other person and what the other person is doing that you deem wrong, you are a bully, not a friend. It is not your job to go around informing the world of other people's mistakes. You need to instead work on you and your own integrity.

Creating Honesty in Others

You might not think you have any control over whether other people are honest with you, but you do. If you are much of the time responding to individuals in a defensive, angry way, they feel that they need to hide situations from you. If you are a jealous person, and you need to hear all the details about your partner's day so that you can feel secure, then you need to be able to control your reactions when you hear communication that you might not like. If you react in a jealous way and demand that your partner never talks to that flirtatious coworker, or even quit that job, your partner is going to stop telling you everything. In fact, you are creating the opposite of what you want. You are causing your partner to be dishonest with you.

You have the ability to create a safe space where a person feels totally secure in being honest with you. All you have to do is trust in yourself, believing that you can handle whatever it is that the other person needs to tell you. To be able to attain this level of confidence in yourself, you need to do a lot of work on you and believe that you have the tools to handle the information that another person could reveal. Much of this will come later in the "Creating Self" chapter. Right now, look at the relationships where you are not receiving answers and see whether you have created a safe enough space for those people to be honest with you.

I had two young-adult girls seek my help about their father, who was having an affair on their mother. They were very upset about the whole affair, and one was taking her father's side because she felt that he was depressed, and the whole family was turning on him. She was nineteen and had been off to college for a while, so she was not witnessing her mother's pain like her older sister, who still lived at home.

The older sister, who was working and living at home, was assuming a caretaking role and was angry at what her father was doing to the family. She tried to talk her mother into kicking him out of the house. She said her mother did not have a job and that in her culture, you didn't kick men out of the house.

I listened to both girls and could see both points or of view and was not going to take a side. Instead, I asked, "What does you dad plan on doing? Does he want to continue the affair or work on the marriage with your mother?"

"I don't know, every time I try to ask him questions, my mom tells me to leave him alone," responded the older sister.

"How are you asking these questions, that your mother feels she needs to defend your father?" I asked sensing that she must be somehow attacking her father.

"Why are you doing this? What do you expect to happen?" She said giving me examples of her questions.

"Do you really care about the answers or are your questions just a way to punish your father for what he has done?" I asked knowing full well what the answer was.

She thought long and hard about this question, and I could tell that she really did want answers.

The family's lives were being turned upside down, and no one was willing to talk about what was going on. She began to see that the way she was asking him the questions was not productive.

"I guess I am trying to punish him, but I'm so mad at him for doing what he did and hurting mom," she confessed.

"Your mother probably knows more of what is going on, and she is trying to protect you, but you have the right to ask questions. You just need to do this in a way that allows your dad to really talk about what is going on. You need to be open to whatever he says and not judge him. I suggest you begin by admitting that you have been judgmental when you have asked questions in the past, but now you are really open to what he has to say. Let him know that you love him, and that is not going to change. Then maybe you will get some answers that you have been looking for that might allow you to understand him and even forgive him. You might also hear things that you don't like as well, but at least you are not left in the dark not knowing."

"Your right!" she said enthusiastically with a new found solution to her problem. "I'll try that!"

It's not wrong to want answers from someone else. It's creating that safe space for someone to share the truth with you that is the key. You might have already lost the other person's trust. This could have to do with how you have handled his or her vulnerability in the past, or it might not have anything to do with you. Whatever has happened in the past, you can now clean it up with that person. Let's say that the other person has opened up to you, and you have held it against him or her over and over. Now you can recognize the moment that you were not open to what the other person said and be responsible for it. You can apologize and make it clear that you are committed to this never happening again.

Maybe you don't trust yourself to handle what the other person has to say. They might say they want out of the relationship, or they don't love you anymore. You might imagine yourself being devastated by these words so you continue to remain in the dark. You are training that person to hold things back from you to avoid devastation. This slowly erodes the relationship and eventually the truth comes out. You feel devastated anyway, but also guilty that you hadn't addressed it earlier in the relationship.

The best way to get over your fears of what they might say is to imagine yourself hearing exactly what you don't want to hear. Imagine yourself responding in a calm way that you can be proud of. Imagine yourself as powerful and capable instead of devastated. If you are still reluctant to ask, have a good friend or coach listen to your fears. Have them play the part of the person you want answers from and have them say whatever you are struggling with hearing. If you end up breaking down, do it again and again until those words no longer have power over you. When you feel that you have faced what you fear and still come out on top, you are then ready to ask for answers.

Trust

Most of us go around looking for someone we can trust that will never let us down. In real life, people do betray us and let us down. It is usually unintentional.

I recently coached a woman who was struggling with trusting either her lover or her friend who said that her partner was trying to come on to her. My coaching was that she only had to look inward and trust herself. Could she accept that this could be going on, or that her friend could be lying to her? Either way was a betrayal from someone, and the person she had to trust was herself. She needed to tap into her intuition about both people and weigh what they were saying. She also needed to believe that she was strong enough to handle any betrayal that came her way. She was able to accept this and make some decisions that empowered her.

There are many ways to increase another's trust in us. One is doing what we say we are going to do and doing it on time. If we say we are going to meet someone for dinner, we need to be there and be on time. Being repeatedly late to events with someone sends a message that this person doesn't matter to us. When we need to break promises, which most of us do sometimes, we need to re-promise or let the person know as soon as possible.

In creating trust, it is important that we not reveal secrets that someone has said to us in confidence. This means that in the heat of an argument, we don't throw back secrets the other person told us in confidence. As others share themselves with us, we need to share ourselves with them and give them personal stories that we have considered sacred, showing that we trust what they will do with this information.

Since most of us are not perfect, it is important that when we are callous and selfish and betray or hurt others, we apologize right away. People make apologies so significant and don't want to admit mistakes. This doesn't have to be so. Although an apology needs to be genuine, it doesn't have to mean that you are incompetent. Apologies are merely admitting that what you did had some influence on someone else. The more we apologize to others, the easier it is for them to apologize to us.

Respect

If you want to have integrity in your relationships, it is important to be respectful at all times. *Respect* is a hard word to define. Every year that I taught school, I would put the word *respect* up, and we would define it as a class. Every class had a slightly different take on what respect looked like. Mostly, I've heard that you should "Do unto others as you would have them do unto you."

This still holds true, but we tend to disregard this when it comes to our spouses or our children. We sometimes consider them as a part of us and expect them to want and need what we want. We may have a life of college, marriage, and two kids already planned for our children, but that may not be what they have envisioned for themselves.

They are separate from us and have different wants and needs. We don't own them. Although they might love and forgive us, it is not okay to take out our frustration on them. They are not there to let us vent and relieve pressure or to take on that negativity that we are exhibiting. This means we should choose our words carefully before speaking. Those times when we are not respectful, and we've suddenly vomited on someone we love with a string of mean words, we need to go back and apologize as soon as possible. We need to make alternative plans for what we are going to do when we are in a mood and want to explode. This could be exercise, meditation, writing down our frustration, or beating a pillow. See what works best for you.

Respect is allowing others to have and express their ideas. People in our lives are there to stretch us and enable us to see different views of life, and we need to hear what they have to say. We might not share their opinions, but we can allow them to have and share their views. My partner and I have separate political beliefs. Instead of starting arguments and debates, I open myself up to his opinions and try to see his point of view. I know that he tries to see my point of view as well. I try to look for where we have common ground with our beliefs and have found that a Democrat and a Republican can cohabitate very well as long as they respect each other's beliefs.

A way of respecting people is to allow them to have lives separate from us. We can't expect other people to always put aside their responsibilities, passions, friends, and hobbies and be with us. People need to recharge. They need the time away to be able to appreciate the time together. If you feel you need to have all of someone else's spare time, this could be unhealthy.

Sacrifices

When we are fair to others in life, we sometimes need to give up past beliefs in order to have that great relationship. The one notion that is sometimes the hardest to give up is that of being right. Our competitive nature loves being right and will cling to it despite the adverse effect on the relationship. In fact, being right can sometimes give people a rush that is better than sex. Dr. Phil has a saying on his show: "Do you want to be right, or do you want to be happy?" Being right can give you a rush in the present, although it later provides you with a hangover that can linger on for many weeks or even years.

So we need to make sacrifices in relationships. That doesn't mean that we totally part from our values. It means that we need to weigh each dispute and decide which fights you want to fight and which ones are not worth it. An example of this is when we play games with our children. Our competitive nature wants to win the game much of the time. If we do, our children might not want to play the game anymore. We might need to lose sometimes in order to allow children to experience winning some in life. I used to play a video game called Dr. Mario with my daughter. I deliberately set my game on a harder setting than hers so that it evened the odds. Sometimes I won, and sometimes she won; nevertheless, it kept her playing with me, and that was more important than winning the game.

Sacrifice can mean giving up the mistakes you have held over your partner's head. It might mean that you can no longer use those mistakes as leverage to obtain what you want from them. Making people live in hell because of mistakes they made is not fair or just. We should not continue to punish them. If you can't give up what a person did, then it might mean that you need to let the person move on to someone else that accepts him or her and does not judge.

Another conviction that we may sacrifice is the belief that we need to control our environment. Managing our environment makes us feel powerful and able to handle any circumstances. Unfortunately, it robs power from others and does not allow them to be able to secure their future. An example of controlling our environment is treating others like they are incapable of handling tasks around the house, managing money, or other such duties.

Whole and Complete

When we were born, we felt at one with our parents and the entire universe. There was no separation between us and others. We felt whole, and we were not broken. Through our experiences in childhood, we began to see ourselves as separate from others. Through criticism, we began to view ourselves as broken and thus unlovable. Through our relationships, we start to seek out the parts of us that we see as missing to feel whole and complete again. During that initial phase of a romantic relationship, we begin to experience that wholeness and the feeling that someone understands us. This is the "falling in love" stage. As this relationship continues, once again we begin to experience the sense of being separate from the other, and we feel that this person was not the one.

Values

So how do we create integrity in relationships? Before we can be honest and fair, or whole and complete, we need to look at what we stand for. We need to know our own values, to know when we or someone else is losing integrity in our eyes. You might not like a person, yet are unsure why. Without the knowledge of your values, you might have difficulty getting to the heart of why you don't like someone. Many times, what a person is doing that perturbs us is what we are fighting with in our own lives.

I found in my own life that after I had discovered my inner victim, I began to hate that side of me and continually fought to destroy that person inside me. In exchange, I became very irritated with others that could not break away from their victim stories. I had no patience and definitely no compassion for them. I knew that compassion would feed their inner victims more, so I mainly walked away from people like that. Being responsible and not a victim is a value that I have, but I need to manage this and have compassion for people who have not yet reached that level of seeing that they can do the same.

Journal activity: Take some time to explore your values. You can google a list of values and then circle and prioritize them. You can ask yourself the following questions:

- What is important to me?
- What do I want to be said about me when I'm dead?
- What irritates me in others?
- What values must my partner have?

Now that you know what your values are, you can take responsibility for your life and your choices. You can make decisions that align with these values. When you are out of integrity, you can look and see what values you are not staying true to. This is where you have the ability to put integrity back into your life. You just acknowledge that what you did or didn't do does not align with what you value. You then go about making promises and setting new actions that will continue to uphold your values.

In relationships, your values and someone else's can come into conflict. Not knowing what a person values and assuming that he or she has the same values as you can be dangerous. If you value organization and your child values inventiveness, you might have a conflict when your very ingenious child is building engines in the front room. This does not mean that you are right, and your child is wrong; it means that you each need to understand where the other is coming from and find a compromise.

This is a time when a couple sees what values they have in common and can begin to make a mission statement about what their relationship or family can stand for. Let's say that a couple discovers that both of them place honesty and abundance in their top ten values. They can then say that the purpose of their relationship is, to be honest and seek wealth. They can post this statement in their house, and when one person wants to spend money behind the other's back, the one who is tempted can think about whether this adds to or subtracts from the integrity of their mission as a couple. I will explore this more in the chapter on commitments.

Remaining Present

Many of us like to dwell on what has passed. We might be holding onto anger or shame about an event that has happened in the past, and that has made us feel broken. We wish it had been different, although we have no power to change what has happened, and thus we are powerless. The pain and suffering can be great, and it affects many aspects of our lives, from our health to our mental state to our relationships.

You may compare what is going on now in your life to your past and miss how life used to be. Maybe you miss the romance that was present in the first year of your marriage, and you want it to go back to that. Perhaps you were athletic, and now you have parts of your body that are no longer capable of doing the athletics you used to do. That feeling of missing the past can cause you to feel pain right now. It can make you feel like you are no longer as wonderful as you used to be.

Thinking entirely about the future can make you not feel whole. Let's say that you fear for your future. You see people getting laid off around you, and you fear that you might soon be without a job. You fear that you will lose all that you have, including your house. You might be fearful about a relationship you are in. You fear that your partner will become bored and leave you, and you knock yourself out trying to take him or her out and come up with activities that you think are entertaining and exciting, purely to keep that person in your life.

You might worry about people you have relationships with. Maybe your son has a drug addiction, and you worry that he will overdose one day. This consumes much of your thoughts, and you have no room to be at peace. You are always checking on him, following him, searching his room, and fighting with him. You are rarely solely present with him and seeing that for today, he is not in jail or dead. Or maybe he is in jail. You can then find peace knowing that for today, he will probably not have access to his drug and overdose. He might someday overdose on his drug; however, you don't have to deal with that until that day comes. Living your life like he is already dead is not positive for the relationship.

You could be thinking about how wonderful life is going to be in the future and comparing it to where you are right now. This longing for a better tomorrow can make you experience pain in your present because you know that you are not yet there. You might want a marriage and child, except right now, you can't secure a second date with someone. You might be thinking that there is some aspect wrong with you, and you will never achieve what you are seeking to achieve.

To feel whole and complete right now can be very peaceful. It takes you seeing that all your experiences that you have had in the past were excellent for creating who you are right now. There was nothing wrong with these experiences; they were all purely lessons in life. You can accept where you are right now as being exactly where you need to be at this moment. Doesn't mean it won't change in the future; however, right now you can be at peace.

There are two things that I do to get present. One method that I use is meditation. I take the time to clear out my thoughts that I am carrying around with me. When I have had a very stressful day and my worries are not going away, I make sure that I meditate until I am at peace again. I have had many ways of meditating: a walk in the mountains, a run on a trail, working out in the gym, being mindful of my breathing, lying under a tree and noticing the details of the leaves, staring at the flicker of a candle, or simply taking a bubble bath with candles where I let go my negativity and bring in the positive energy. I have sat and meditated with guided meditation or with mantras. How you meditate does not matter as long as you bring your thoughts to what is happening right now at this moment.

Another method I use is grace. When I am grateful for what I have at this time, I experience being present as well as peace. I have heard that you can't have negativity and grace in the same space, so simply going through a list of circumstances that I am grateful for makes me feel whole and complete in the moment. I have found this to be very helpful when I am trying to go to sleep. It becomes somewhat of a prayer in which I thank God for all he has shown me or given me that day. I am thankful for the people in my life, the possessions that I have acquired, and the accomplishments that I achieved that day. This wasn't always the case. I used to go to bed worried about what the next day would hold or upset about an event that had happened during the day. My mind would be racing, and I felt like I had to solve the problem before going to sleep. I would toss and turn for hours, and when I did sleep, I would have nightmares about my problem. I have found that listing many of the circumstances that I'm grateful for in my head has made me obtain much more rest than in the past.

Created Communication

Most of our communication is not created. It can be patterned that we repeat every day. You automatically say things and forget them immediately without a second thought. This is why your partner needs to remind you of items that one or the other of you said. We are poor listeners as well, and either we are in our own heads thinking about other issues or we are planning on what we are going to say next before the other person has had the chance to finish. We relate what we are hearing to a communication that we have heard before and begin assuming we know what is being said. Sometimes a communication will be a trigger for us that sends us into the fight, flight, or freeze mode. Many times, our communication is not straightforward; we expect the other person to read our minds, and we are not stating what we want or need.

Patterned Communication

We go through life communicating with the same patterns. "Hi." "Good morning." "How are you?" Many times, we ask questions of others and don't care to hear the answers to these. These are some of the niceties that we exchange during the day to avoid being rude. Unfortunately, these patterned communications don't allow us to intimately interact with the other people.

I had a discovery about the phrase *thank you* one day. I noticed that *thank you* was simply a nicety that I threw around because it was ingrained in me as politeness as a child. When I thought about what *thank you* actually meant, which was an acknowledgment of what someone was doing for me, I began to put my intention on it whenever I said it. I wanted the people I said it to to feel acknowledged. I did this with strangers as they opened up the door for me, for the cashier who rang up the food at the register, and to the waitperson at a restaurant that brought me my food or poured me a refill.

Beginning to notice our random communications can be an awakening. We start to see what we are saying and how asleep we are as we say those things. We are not mentally present for many of our conversations, and the people we are conversing with are not awake as well. We walk through life being in our own heads and not connecting to the many lovely people around us. Thus, we feel separate and alone and not connected; however, we are the ones creating that. This is not necessarily so. When I began to show my presence around the phrase *thank you,* I could see that it was affecting others. I could tell that because they would give me a smile and sometimes a warm "You're welcome."

We have patterns of communication that were ingrained in us as children. We might repeat these same patterns to our own children that were repeated to us. Thus we pass down patterns of communication from generation to generation. An example of this could be that when we first see them in the morning, we might say, "Did you make your bed?" or "Did you brush your teeth?" This might not be a value that is important to us; however, these questions have been patterned into us since we were children, and they are automatic. Our kids will then go on to use these same patterns with their children. This is why many generations continued with "Children should be seen not heard." Patterns can be seen and then changed, and we don't have to carry them forward. With created communication, you begin to notice which patterns are beneficial and align with your values, and which ones are not useful and could be conveying opinions you don't believe.

My daughter one day got angry with me for asking questions. I was frustrated with this because I thought that was the one way of connecting with her and showing that I cared about her life. I then began to notice the questions that I was asking, and I noticed that they were not simple questions that showed my interest in her. They were veiled questions that showed my judgments of how she was living her life. They were questions that were trying to force her to see her life the way I did. These questions were things like "Don't you care that you smell like marijuana at your job?" and "Does your boyfriend help you out financially?" (When I suspected that he didn't.) I saw that I was not actually accepting her for who she was; Instead, I tried to impose my values on to her and fix her. I had to be conscious of the questions that I asked her, and I had to refrain from asking her questions for a while because I wasn't sure myself which ones were veiled and which ones were not.

These patterns don't solely arise with our children. They can happen with anyone. You should begin to notice your patterns with your partner or your employees. Are you always nagging them about issues? Are you not caring about how their day is going, or who they are as people? One simple "How are your kids?" where you genuinely want to know can be very endearing to an employee and make him or her want to work harder for you. This can be more productive than the nagging that goes in one ear and out the other.

Journal activity: Notice what you say to people automatically and what your intent is saying those things. Journal about this and find the ones that you would like to change. Begin to change up what you say to others and show presence when you say these new things. See what reactions you gain from them.

Patterned Communication to Self

Just as we have patterned communication with others, we have internal dialogues going on in our heads that will repeat the same discourse over and over. Many times, this automatic patterned dialogue is not kind to self. Much of this dialogue is repeating what someone told us in childhood, and we repeat it over and over—sayings like "I'm stupid," "I'm not pretty," "I can't," and "I'm alone." When we do this, we are creating how others treat us. If we think that we are stupid, then others begin to see us as stupid as well—or even when they see us as smart, they are unable to convey this to us because we already have an image of ourselves as stupid.

The patterned communication to self is the hardest to overcome because it has been running in the background for a long time. We have been creating it in our relationships and finding others that validate our internal dialogue. If I have the internal dialogue that "I can't" playing in my brain, I will find people who do tasks for me. I become needy, and I surround myself with people that believe I'm weak and can't solve my own problems. When I try to break out of this pattern, I will have anxiety and stress because I have internally come to believe that "I can't."

One way to transform these negative messages is to note that this is not you that is talking and thinking this way. This is some patterned tape in your brain. It takes over when you are on automatic pilot and not creating what you want to think or believe. At first, when you hear this voice, simply notice it and listen to what it is saying. Then begin to challenge it and ask yourself "Is that true?" In most cases, you will be able to find empowering messages that contradict the negative ones that are going on inside your brain. You can create a new way of thinking and replace those messages. Instead of thinking "I can't," try replacing it with "I haven't." This is true and still leaves the door open to actually trying. You can begin to picture yourself having accomplished endeavors and how this feels.

There are days when the inner voice is going crazy. You can't force it to shut up. Usually, this happens when you are stressed, or some negative events are going on in your life. With me, there are times when my brain feels that there is a problem, and I have to somehow resolve this issue, and it will not rest until I do. I have two practices that I use when my brain is on blab mode.

One practice I use is meditation. I spoke about meditation as a way to get present. I also find it is wonderful for quieting my inner dialogue. It is especially fantastic for clearing out my brain when my brain is going haywire. When my brain is in stress mode, I might need more than a quiet place to meditate. I might need a candle that I keep bringing my focus back to and watching the flames dance. I might need to sit under my tree out back and experience the beauty of nature around me.

A second practice I use is journaling. I will begin writing down the negative thoughts that are taking over my brain. I then create a character that argues with those beliefs and creates new scenarios that are not as negative. I go on and on with this until I begin to believe the most positive side. Here is an example of this.

Negative Self: My coworkers at work didn't invite me to lunch with them. They must not like me.

Positive Self: Are you sure that is true?

Negative Self: Yes, they made it clear right in front of me that they were all going to a restaurant, and they made sure that they had invited everyone on the team but did not say a word to me.

Positive Self: How do you know that they didn't simply forget to invite you or merely assumed that if you wanted to go, you would only tag along?

Negative Self: Why would they make it a point to ask others and not me? *(I begin to waver here and repeat myself.)*

Positive Self: Didn't they overhear you talking to your boyfriend about lunch? Maybe they assumed you already had lunch planned and wouldn't want you to feel guilty about telling them no.

Negative Self: So you are saying that they were actually caring about my feelings instead of excluding me?

Positive Self: Yes, but you could ask them if you want to.

Negative Self: No, I'll take your word for it.

Sometimes I don't have to write this kind of scenario down. It sometimes begins to happen in my head automatically as I consciously create my inner dialogue. The more practice that I have had with this kind of dialogue, the quicker this process goes.

Journal activity: Write down the dialogue that you say to yourself and notice whether the voice is being your biggest fan or your worst enemy. Begin seeing the voice for what it is, which is purely a voice and not literally who you are. Then begin to transform these thoughts. You could try the back-and-forth dialogue that I used in the preceding section.

Listening

When you are genuinely listening to a person, it can be the one way that you show them that you actually do love them. Scott Peck once said, "True listening, total concentration on the other, and is always a manifestation of love." Real listening takes effort. It requires clearing your head and deeply listening to the person without judgment and without the need to take the conversation somewhere.

Setting time aside requires stopping whatever you are doing and putting your attention on the individual who is talking. When there have been problems in a relationship, sometimes a time set aside to do this is needed. It might seem phony to set aside time to talk, but it is beneficial.

In my own relationship, my need for this kind of attention is usually when I first see my partner. I need to talk about my day right away. This might include talking about what I learned, or sometimes I need to complain about some event to get it off my chest. Simply talking about what excites me or upsets me gives me the space to be with my partner for the rest of the day and be present. He understands this, and he is there for me. He lets me begin talking the minute one of us comes through the door. He asks questions that show he is interested in what I say. In this way, I feel heard.

The next method that is important in deeply listening is to accept the person for who he or she is and not judge what he or she is saying. Sometimes this can be difficult, especially with your children. If your kids are doing activities that you don't approve of and they are talking about it in front of you, you might have a hard time listening to them. You might want to go into a fixing mode and try to influence them to see the error of their ways. This doesn't allow them to feel accepted and listened to. This furthers your own agenda. This teaches them that there are some subjects that they can talk to you about and some subjects that they need to stay away from. This does not allow them to truly be open with you and trust you.

Intent listening involves putting yourself into another's shoes. A recent movie came out called *The Cobbler,* in which Adam Sandler plays a shoe repairman that has the ability to step into a man's shoes and be and see life from his point of view. We don't need this kind of magic to discover what is going on in someone else's head; we simply need to give up who we think that person is and sincerely listen openly to see if we can experience what that person's point of view is. When we get into the other person's world and validate what he or she is trying to say, this opens up communication, and the person feels truly heard.

Truly listening is hearing what the other person is saying, noticing the emotion with which he or she is saying it, and looking for the commitment behind the communication. In non-created communication, we are solely hearing our own sides and not getting into the other's world. We then feel hurt and feel the other person is doing more to hurt us. The following is an example of a non-created communication.

Geno arrives home two hours late and walks through the door saying, "I'm so sorry I'm late. They offered me two hours of overtime pay to help train someone on the next shift, and I took it."

Jenna retorts angrily, "Likely story! Who is this girl you are sleeping with?"

Geno steps back as if he had suddenly been slapped in the face and responds angrily, "Why do you always think that I'm with someone else? I just wanted to make some extra money!"

"I've heard that story before, and I'm not falling for it again. You're cheating, and you should just tell me, so we can move on with our lives!"

"Jenna, I don't know how I can convince you that I'm not cheating, and if you can't trust me, I don't see how this marriage will ever work!" he yells at her as he turns to leave again.

"Go ahead and choose your tramp over me and see if I care," she retorts as she begins sobbing.

In this scenario, we as outsiders can see that Jenna is committed to not being left in the dark again in her relationships. Geno is not a cheater; his commitment is to support his family and Jenna financially. Both are in their own worlds and not understanding the other's point of view. If Geno had taken a moment to breathe and to come at this from deeply understanding Jenna instead of defending his point of view, this scenario could have gone like this.

Geno arrives home two hours late and walks through the door saying, "I'm so sorry I'm late. They offered me two hours of overtime pay to help train someone on the next shift, and I took it."

Jenna retorts angrily, "Likely story! Who is this girl you are sleeping with?"

Geno sees that she is angry and in pain and knows that his staying at work late has triggered Jenna and brought up wounds of being hurt in the past. He takes a breath and, with compassion for her instead of anger, recreates her communication. He stays calm and says, "I see that my being late has made you angry and hurt, and it is making you believe that I'm with another woman."

"Yes, who is she?"

"I know that men have betrayed you in your past, and you hate being lied to. It is hard for you to see when someone is faithful, but I would never do that to you, and I would be honest with you if I did."

"How do I know that?" she asks as she begins to calm down and feel his concern for her. "How do I know that you are not lying to me now?"

Geno understands that she struggling to trust him and wants to believe him, but does not want to be duped again. He responds once again with compassion, "You are fighting to trust me, and you want to believe me, but you are scared that you will become hurt again. I understand that, and there is not much I can do to convince you of this because you have probably heard it all before. I'm committed to this marriage, and I'm committed that one day you have trust in me, no matter how long this takes."

The preceding scenario required work on Geno's part to stay present with Jenna and to not let Jenna's arrows that she was slinging at him stick. After working two extra hours at his job, the last thing he wanted to do was to have to work at his relationship. Solely spending some time getting into Jenna's world and indeed seeing what she was dealing with took effort. Showing a commitment to the healing of another's wounds can make a huge difference in relationships.

Some of you might think that you don't have the ability to get into another's world. You weren't born with that psychic ability to feel what another feels or think what another thinks. I'm telling you that it is innate within many of us, and it is our job to recognize this and take the reins to break the pattern. When I worked in a homeless shelter for teens, I could come in in the morning and right away pick up on the chaos from the night before. I could feel the frustration from the night staff as well as the anger and fear of the teens. I could then choose to feel the frustration, anger, or fear as well and continue to have a crazy day, or I could consciously choose to shift the energy and emotions of the house through remaining calm and solely listening to what was going on. I would start by allowing the night staff the chance to vent, plus ensure them that I was now there to take over and calm the environment down. I would then start a group where the teens could say whatever they had to say and know that I was going to deeply listen to them and stand for their peace of mind and their safety. Just listening to someone and letting them get it all out is what it takes to be a good listener. Asking questions such as "Is there more?" or "What else happened?" can start to let a person release the pressure that was building up inside them.

To remain calm, present and not become part of the problem relies on us knowing our triggers.

Triggers

Triggers stop us from genuinely listening to others and seeing what they are committed to. Triggers are misfortunes that happen in life that cause an emotional response within us. Many times, the emotional response causes us to not be fully present with others. Triggers can keep us trapped in the same kinds of communication that are not useful to us. Sometimes the people in our lives know our triggers. They are able to say absolutely the right thing that will send us over the edge, and then we lose what we wanted to accomplish or say during a communication. I spoke about this in the chapter on responsibility. Now I want to elaborate more on it in relation to communication.

Being able to recognize our own triggers and notice that someone is pushing those buttons becomes half the battle to overcoming these obstacles. I was caught in a cycle for many years with my ex-husband. People will tell you that you should simply divorce your spouse and flee an unhappy marriage. They don't realize that getting out doesn't necessarily end the unhealthy cycle of a relationship and can make it worse. I had two children with my ex-husband, and I had to see him and communicate with him quite a bit. He had many years of finding my triggers, as did I with him. Our interactions were full of us pushing each other's buttons. All he had to do was to criticize my abilities as a mother, and I was off and running, criticizing his abilities as a father. We had years of court battles over the children, arguments over the telephone that ended with slammed receivers, and times when we were not talking to each other at all.

One day, I decided that I was not going to fight with him anymore. I recognized that he was able to get under my skin every time he criticized me as a parent, and this time, I was going to let it go through me without sticking. No matter what, I wasn't going to throw back my own daggers. I started with one of those difficult conversations where I took responsibility. I called him up and said, "I realized today that I have not been letting you be a father to our girls. I always criticize you as a dad. I whisk the children away whenever they have a conflict with you because I don't trust you to be able to handle it. I thank you for giving me these two wonderful daughters. I will always love you for that reason. I am no longer going to fight with you."

There was dead silence on the other side of the phone. He didn't know what to say to this and just thanked me.

The next time I saw him, he was late and immediately defensive. "How come the girls aren't ready? I'm already late and going to be even later."

I was determined not to fight with him, so I just danced in the conversation. "You are right, the girls should be ready, how can I help you get them ready?"

He looked at their messy room and said, "You should make these girls clean their rooms."

I believed in natural consequences and allowing the girls to keep the room the way they saw fit. So I just responded with "I see that a clean room is important to you and me. I hope the girls catch on to that as well."

"You were never that clean when we were married either," he said with satisfaction knowing this was one of my triggers.

I just laughed and responded, "Are you trying to get me to fight with you? If you are, it's not working. I told you that I will not fight with you anymore." "Why are their rooms being clean so important to you?" I asked with a new found curiosity about his values. Eventually, the criticism stopped, and he began to listen to me as well. We got committed to being in a partnership for our children despite our inability to agree with each other.

I couldn't have been able to accomplish this without looking at my triggers. Many times, our triggers center around not being good enough. We have beliefs inside ourselves that we must be broken or not good enough, and when others say what we already believe about ourselves, it will trigger us. If we didn't already believe what people said, they would not affect us. If someone calls me a hippo and I know myself to be a healthy weight and beautiful, it does not affect me in the slightest, and I can react curiously as to why they said this. On the other hand, if I have been struggling with my weight and someone calls me a hippo, I become hurt and might react in many negative ways.

Journal activity: Write down the experiences that cause you to have emotional reactions and make you react in a way that you regret. What beliefs do you have around these experiences? Why do you hold these beliefs about yourself or others? Make a commitment that you will no longer allow others to control you.

Communicating Wants and Needs

Knowing What You Want

When you are having your wants and needs met in a relationship, you find satisfaction in that relationship, and the relationship grows. Where relationships die is where you are not getting your needs met and you might be giving and giving and not receiving. This could mean that you are not communicating what your wants and needs are in this relationship in a way that is being heard and honored. Before you can communicate these, you first have to know what you want.

It is not easy to know what you actually want out of a relationship. We as children are sometimes brought up to not ask for items, and we start to deny what we think we need. You might believe that you don't deserve what you want. Our society has convinced us to want material items, but these are not necessarily what we need. Most of us have emotional needs such as love, respect, acceptance, security, appreciation, and attention. We think we need romance, diamonds, and expensive vacations.

Once again, if you are asleep in the relationship and letting it happen, you are not aware of what is going on. In a created relationship, you begin to notice your feelings when you are with someone. Our feelings are what call to us and try to wake us up to what we are lacking. These might be different with different people. With your children, you might be lacking respect. With your boss, it might be appreciation. With your partner, it might be attention. To give us direction on our needs you must look at either what you are complaining about or the issues you argue over. Inside of all these are a hidden need for something.

Sometimes you need to look below the surface and see what is lacking. You might be complaining that you never have any help around the house; however, you won't let anyone help. What you might really be lacking is an appreciation for what you are doing around the house. Maybe at work, your complaint is that you didn't receive the promotion that you wanted, but the real issue is that you lack security.

When I read *The Five Love Languages* by Gary Chapman, it opened my world up to why neither my ex-husband nor I felt satisfied in our relationship. We had different definitions of love and were not filling each other's "love tanks." I wanted and needed attention through quality time, and he was a physical love person. I wanted to talk when he got home. He just wanted to sit in front to the television and get his back scratched. Neither one of us were getting our needs met, so we withheld from the other. No wonder our marriage failed. He and I read this book after we had already divorced and were able to apologize and laugh about our missed opportunities within the marriage. While exploring your wants and needs, I do suggest you either read *The Five Love Languages* or go online and take the quiz.

Journal activity: List the people in your life and rate your satisfaction within each relationship on a scale of one to ten. Ask yourself "What is my complaint with them? What are we repeatedly arguing over?" Look to see what might be missing in the relationship that you might need to ask for.

Asking for What You Want

About ten years ago, I discovered that what stopped me in life was that I could not ask for what I wanted. It stemmed from being a child and being told that if I asked for items, I was not going to get them. In fact, if my parents thought I was whining about not getting the toy, the candy, or the new shoes, I was punished. If I wanted to go somewhere or do some activity with my friends, I was only allowed to ask once, and then I had to wait patiently until my mother made a decision. Many times, I missed out on opportunities while waiting. This taught me that the objects

I wanted didn't matter, or that I needed to manipulate people to get them.

I found that if I hinted at what I wanted, sometimes I could get it. As an adult, I actually surrounded myself with people whom I rarely needed to ask for anything. All I had to do was hint about what I wanted or tell these people my problems, and they would offer to help.

This way of manipulating people only got me so far in my life. Not everyone—especially not my students, coworkers, or extended family—understood my wants from my hints. Some people figured that I was okay with the status quo if I didn't ask for what I wanted. I began to see a need to ask for what I wanted although it terrified me. I have found that my problem is not unique. Many of us as children were not allowed to ask for what we wanted. We seem to be afraid of that ghastly word *no*. We appear to equate the word *no* with many negative beliefs like thinking the other person doesn't love us or respect us, or that we are imposing on the other person. I've heard the saying, "It never hurts to ask," although, for many of us, it is agonizing to ask. The more importance we give to what we are asking for, the more afraid we are of asking for it. A proposal of marriage can be one of the scariest questions a person can ask someone.

We go through life expecting others to be psychic and know what we want and need: "I shouldn't have to tell him that I want an apology; he should know what he did and apologize for it." We withdraw and withhold our love, waiting for that person to know what we want, and in reality, that person has no clue why we are withdrawing. We then move on to that next person, who we feel profoundly understands our wants and needs. We may find that for a little while because people at the beginning of relationships are trying to be impressive, and will do many different kinds of actions to impress a new partner. They will eventually fall over the answer. They have no clue what the other person wants or needs. No one has the stamina to keep this up for very long, and it begins to look like they no longer care. Instead of moving from relationship to relationship, you might as well start asking for what you need and want in your current relationship.

So how do you do this?

1. Be clear what you want before the conversation.
2. Be clear why you have this want so that you can explain it.
3. Expect a positive outcome and have the confidence that the person you are talking to is concerned about you getting your needs met as well.
4. Find a time and place that is good for the both of you so that you can explore the topic.
5. Ask for what you want in a clear, Asking for what you want.
6. Listen carefully to their response and be willing to negotiate. He or she might have something they want in the process.
7. Look for ways that both of you can get what you want.

Journal activity: Be in action and go out and ask for something every day for a week. Look at how you are asking. Where you are expressive with asking, and where are you stopped?

Created Commitment

Commitment

a : an agreement or pledge to do something in the future, especially an engagement to assume a financial obligation at a future date

b : something pledged

c : the state or an instance of being obligated or emotionally impelled (a commitment to a cause)

Hidden Commitments

You may not feel you have any commitments in your life, or you may feel like you avoid commitments. You have them all the same. You are emotionally impelled to do many actions in your life. If you are avoiding commitments because you don't want any obligations hanging over your head, you are committed to avoiding commitments. Avoiding commitments becomes your cause that you believe in.

When looking at what your commitments are, what you need to do is look at what you are spending your time and your attention on. You can have many commitments that you had not intended to have. You might spend a lot of time playing Facebook games or watching reality shows, and your cause would be to escape, relax, or crush one more candy.

We want to say that we have noble commitments, like to our family or to our partners. Unfortunately, when we look at our commitments, how much time are we actually spending with our families? How much attention are you giving to your partner? If you spend eighty hours a week at your job and say that you are committed to your family, what you are absolutely committed to might be looking good at work, financial stability, or any number of causes. It is not your relationship with your family.

I might say that I am committed to my health, but if I'm not spending time eating right and exercising, I'm actually committed to doing what I want and eating whatever I want. Your commitments should be based on your values that you looked at in chapter three on integrity. If they're not, you can feel like you are not making a difference in the world, and you are not acting on what you believe is valuable in life.

I'm not saying that we have to always have commitments that others see as redeemable and based on your values. I admit that during the *Walking Dead* season, I'm committed to the show. I watch every episode the minute it comes on, I talk about it with anyone who is interested, and I schedule my life around watching this show at the time that it is on. What is not happening is that it is a commitment that is running in my background. It is an intentional commitment that I know about and can be responsible for. I'm committed that it has enough viewers that it continues to be on television.

Relationships require commitment. They require you to pledge yourself to making them work and going about filling your obligations in the relationship so that they can last. You need to be able to create and keep those commitments, or the people in your life begin to feel you are not committed to them and willing to make them a priority. The biggest commitment that runs in the background of many people is the commitment of doing what they want when they want. This can work for you if you don't have a job or people who depend on you. It doesn't work with those you love.

Journal activity: What are your feelings toward the word commitment? What are some things that you spend your time doing that you can now see as a hidden commitment?

Obligations

Obligations can seem like a burden. They are usually authorities that rule outside ourselves and dictate what we must do, and since we were two years old, we have been avoiding having people tell us what we should or shouldn't do. We are rebellious beings, and we hate the feelings of obligations. Some obligations we live with because they are a part of life, such as paying our bills or taking out the trash, but we don't love these obligations.

Many of us avoid more relationships because we don't want to be obligated to go to more events, or to listen to others when they call or help them when they move. We begin to close ourselves off from the world more and more until the only serious relationship we have is with our pets, who do not have any expectations from us. Our pets love us unconditionally, and many of us wish our human relationships could be as uncomplicated as our relationships with our pets. Well before you find a secluded house and become the next big cat lady, you need to know that there is freedom and joy in creating obligations that fulfill you and make you want to do them. Not because you should do them but because if you don't, you are not fulfilling your purpose in the world.

Created Commitments versus Hidden

Created commitments are different from hidden ones because you are intentionally creating them and overcoming your fear of failure or your avoidance of obligation to make sure that your commitments come to fruition. Created commitments are ones that give you energy, not sap it. They have nothing to do with "doing what you want when you want" because they have a purpose that you are committed to fulfilling. Created commitments call you into powerfully challenging your feelings of "I don't want to" via becoming present to what you are passionately committed to. Fears drive hidden commitments such as looking good at work, whereas created commitments can cause you to powerfully face your fears because you start to see yourself as unstoppable.

Created commitments can create partnerships where you and others are working toward a cause. Hidden commitments avoid partnerships. Created commitment to someone's success is the makings of true love and giving so that the other person feels supported and valued. Created commitments do not always have a path that is straightforward, and we don't always know how to fulfill our created commitments. The intentionality that is involved in a created commitment can be uplifting and powerful. Hidden commitments are hidden, and sometimes you are not aware of what they are. Created commitments are shared with others bravely so that others can hold you to your word. Created commitments don't let fear get in the way, and hidden commitments are usually based on fear.

What Do You Want in Your Life?

To be able to create robust commitments, we need to look at what we want in life. Part of my daily meditation is spent on contemplating what I want. It allows me to deeply think about what I want in my life, and this keeps my commitments in my forefront on a daily basis, so that I don't leave my house without knowing my commitments. If I don't keep my commitments in my present thoughts, the hidden commitments take over, and I end up with another day of doing what I want, when I want.

Many people feel that they should be grateful for all they have right now and not want more in life. Being grateful for what is in front of you is extraordinary. It is not selfish to want more, though. Human beings are wired to want more in their lives. More love, more money, more happiness, more joy, and more relationships are what people crave.

As you are looking for yourself and what you want more of, you can think about others and what they want. Sometimes wanting others to not be homeless is as rewarding as wanting a new car, if not more rewarding. You probably want better relationships with someone in your life, and that is what brought you to this book in the first place.

Journal activity: Finish this sentence-"What I really want in life is ...." Keep writing things down until you have nothing left to say.

What Is the Purpose of Your Life?

I meditate daily on what my purpose is in life. It grounds me in what I feel I do in life that is valuable to others. Purpose does not necessarily have to be about one's career, although it can. I know that one of my purposes in life is to teach. I'm masterful at it, and I do it through either writing, coaching, or teaching my students how to read. It's my calling as well as being a mother and a partner. Each day when I meditate on my purpose, it will sometimes change or vary somewhat, and that is okay with me. I might have a purpose to fulfill in that one day.

You might be struggling with what you feel your purpose is. Some of that angst might be from thinking that you are limited to one purpose in life and that this one purpose is hidden from you. To find a purpose, ask, "What can I do right now that is important?" This might be linked to activities that you are skilled at or causes you feel passionate about. This is up to you. Some purposes, as you can find, call on you instead of you creating them.

When I was in high school, I wanted to be a park ranger. I did shadowing of park rangers, and I spent a summer in Yellowstone with some unique rangers. What I discovered was that many park rangers wanted to be teachers. When I looked at the reasons I wanted to be a park ranger, it was because I wanted to teach people about the park, nature, and the history of the park. I didn't like the idea of having to carry a gun, give tickets, cut down trees, and undertake some of the other tasks that a ranger did. I finally decided that what I indeed wanted to do was to teach.

When I decided that teaching was the profession for me, I thought that being an English teacher was the best fit because I loved reading and writing. After years of trying to find a position as an English teacher, I ended up teaching English in a detention center and discovered my gifts of working with troubled youth and with students who struggled with academics as well. I had predicted this because I was inexperienced with people with disabilities. I later had a daughter with a learning disability, and it was completely synchronistic that I had already learned much about the field. Had I not been aware of myself and open to changes in my life, I might not have seen my purpose as a special education teacher. I might have given up on teaching altogether in the years when I struggled to find a job.

Looking at your purpose in life is looking at what you might have quite a bit of passion for. Maybe it is a cause that you can't seem to shake. Maybe it is some accomplishment that you said you were going to do as a child, yet have since given up on as you became resigned in life. Maybe it is a legacy you want to leave behind you on this earth so that people know that you once existed. Whatever it could be, you need to claim it and not let fear talk you out of it.

Journal activity: Finish this sentence-"My purpose in life is ...." Keep writing each purpose until you have nothing left to say.

Creating Commitments

Now that you have looked at your wants and your purpose in life, it is time to create your commitments. What is it that you want to intentionally obligate yourself toward? What promise do you want to fulfill in your life? Currently, I have commitments toward inspiring others to find their power, financial stability, adventure, and having amazing relationships. Out of these commitments, I will create my obligations or goals, such as finishing this book, saving money for retirement, going to Paris, and setting aside time for my friends, family, and partner. To make these goals a reality and not merely a pipe dream, I will make promises to myself and others that I will fulfill these goals. Each day as obstacles arise—and if you want to live a big life, you are going to experience enormous obstacles—I need once again to remember what I am committed to. If all I had were goals, I might work on them or not during that day. As commitments, I am always noticing whether I am fulfilling them or ignoring them. If I am moving away from my commitment, then the commitment has changed.

When you have created commitments, you surround yourself with reminders of your commitments. I have vision boards, pictures, and calendars of places that I want to see in my office. I have pictures of lovers in my bedroom as a constant reminder of how it feels to be in love and feel loved. I have sayings on my walls that encourage me with what I am committed to. There is no way that I can forget my commitments in my life because I surround myself with them.

Journal activity: What are some commitments do you are you creating from reading this book? What are some actions that you can take to keep these commitments in front of you?

Intentional Scheduling

Commitments are not significant without having actions around them. You should have lists of tasks to fulfill your commitments. If you are committed to having a better relationship with your family, begin scheduling quality time when you can intensely give the attention that you have meant to give to the people you love. Plan your vacations and absolutely commit to making the time off happen despite what your boss is expecting you to do. Once you schedule these activities, share this plan with your family and don't mess with it.

Maybe you are committed to some charitable project where you are helping others in a meaningful way; begin scheduling actions around this. Call people and let them know what you are doing, and obtain a group of people to help out on the project. This can be beneficial if you are committed to having more friends around you.

Maybe you are committed to having a better sex life with your partner. Begin having discussions around this as well and planning a time when you can try new techniques that will enhance your sex.

Maybe having a loving partner, marriage, and a family is what you are committed to. You might need to schedule some dates and begin looking into what has been standing in your way to having this. Maybe you need to schedule a breakup with the current partner who has the counter-commitment of not being married or having a family.

Journal activity: Instead of your journal, grab your calendar and begin scheduling the actions that you created.

Created Partnerships

Because created commitments are shared, you need to begin thinking who you want to share them with. You might have wondered what commitment is doing in a book on relationships. You need to have those people in your corner that believe in you and believe in your commitments to help you to achieve your goals. If you keep your ideas to yourself, they are purely excellent ideas and probably never going to be more than ideas. As you begin to tell others in your life what you are committed to, you are no longer able to back out of the deal. Others now see you making promises, and they expect you to fulfill your obligations. This takes risk because we don't always know who will believe in us, and we don't always believe in ourselves enough to make these promises. Remember that you don't always know how you are going to fulfill the commitment. It's the intention that counts. Many times, when I share my commitments, people want to help and want to give me advice on how to achieve what I'm out to achieve. The saying "Two heads are better than one" goes without saying. Having a group of people is better because you end up having many ideas out there.

Journal activity: Who are the people in your life that would be willing to help you with your commitment? What questions do you want to ask them? What requests do you want to make of them?

Overcoming Obstacles

As you create robust commitments that leave you fully alive, you will experience powerful obstacles. You might take off like a rocket on a project or commitment, and then one negative comment from someone else will have you plummeting to the earth and out of control. You might go back to school to earn a degree, and one bad grade leaves you doubting that you will ever accomplish your dreams. Maybe you finally decided to commit to a relationship and marry, but the person you wanted to spend the rest of your life with refuses your proposal. Perhaps you are committed to making your marriage work, and your partner serves you with divorce papers. These are enormous obstacles, although they don't have to defeat you. Maybe you are committed to having a beautiful and fruitful marriage, except your current partner, might not be the one. The commitment is still there. You might have to wait for a committed partner.

Whatever obstacles you face, you need to believe that they are there to challenge your commitments and to indeed make you stronger in your commitment.

Created Self

Before any of us can be in a healthy relationship, we ought to be healthy ourselves. We need to truly love who we are. We only allow people to abuse us when we don't value that person that we have become. We hold on to shame, guilt, and loathing for the person we are and then expect others to love us. We go through our lives giving much of what we have worked for to others and keeping none of it for ourselves, and we end up finding people that will take and take and not give back. If we have true love for ourselves, others cannot hold us hostage with their love. If they give us love, that is wonderful; if they take it away, that is wonderful as well because we continue to love ourselves. When we are at our healthiest selves, we attract others that are healthy. If you are in a romantic relationship and you feel that it is not healthy, working on yourself can be highly beneficial to the relationship and can either cause a shift in the relationship itself or cause the relationship to dissolve so that you can both move on to what fits the new you. Your partner might be happy that the focus is on transforming you and not trying to fix him or her.

Belief That You Are Broken

When you were born, you were whole and perfect emotionally. You had no thoughts of how you weren't good enough; you were purely alive and happy. Life revolved around you. When you cried, someone fed, held, or changed you, and that was how life was. When you got older and life did not quite go how you expected, you began to think that it was your fault. Maybe you didn't get fed right away when you were hungry, so you might have thought that your mother no longer loved you as much as she used to. When your brother or sister came along, you began to think that your parents loved the new sibling more than they loved you. Maybe you broke some priceless object and you got punished for it, and you began to believe that you were clumsy and stupid. When people were critical of you, you believed them to be telling you the truth.

You believed what others said, and then you began collecting evidence of your beliefs. If you thought you were stupid, you noticed mistakes you made or grades that were unsatisfactory. You actually ignored the excellent grades. When that first boy or girl rejected you, you began to think that you were unlovable. These are some of the beliefs that children pick up when they are young. I've known children who were abused by their parents physically and believed that if someone was hitting them, this was because the abuser loved them. I knew a boy once at the homeless shelter for teens who had been physically and emotionally abused, and he went around harassing other students, telling on them, taunting them, or irritating them in other ways until someone would haul off and hit him. He refused to fight back when he was hit. He solely took it, and I could see that he was much like an abused wife taunting her man into hitting her so that she could feel loved by him.

My daughter dated a guy who was much of the time putting himself down. He went to great pains to make my daughter intensely angry with him and then got to play the victim when she would yell at him. Once when she was out with him, he got severely ill and went to the ER. My daughter was frightened and called me. I went to the hospital to be her support and sat in the waiting room with his parents. They were constantly saying rude things about him even as the doctors were in the next room trying to save his life. I suddenly realized what the poor boy had been raised with, and it was no wonder that he saw himself the way he did.

If you see yourself as broken, you will allow people to treat you poorly. You will feel it is normal, or you will feel that you deserve the way you are treated. No one deserves to be mistreated. You didn't deserve it as a child, and you don't deserve it now.

Being Taken Advantage Of

If you had to take care of someone when you were a child, you might think that you need to take care of people as an adult. You might have had a parent who was not capable of caring for you or your siblings, or you might have felt like you had to take care of a parent who was an alcoholic or incapacitated by some illness.

You might think that your destiny is to care for others, and you feel noble doing this. This is fine if you don't feel like you are being used in the process. Some people love to prey on people that care for others. They might expect you to always take care of them or pay their bills. If this is the case, then you are feeling drained when you help others, not fulfilled. You feel drained because you know that they are not appreciative, are not doing anything for themselves, and are solely relying on you.

If you have enough love for them and for yourself, you will make sure that people are not taking advantage of you.

Steps to Metamorphosis

Before you can ever transform yourself and your relationships, you need to have a willingness to change. This takes digging down deep and seeing that you no longer want to accept the way your life is. This could be as a result of a breakup or the result of stirrings to break out of a relationship or marriage. This could be from being tired of the pain you have been going through and feeling the need for a change. This can stem from the realization that your relationship is not what you wanted. It's accepting that although you might not be able to change other people, you surely can start becoming healthy yourself and no longer allow abuse from others.

Change takes courage, and although we wish that others around us would change to make our lives happy, we know that it is not their responsibility to make us happy. It is our own responsibility to do that.

The first step to becoming healthy is to look at the areas that are working and not working. You need to then begin to take each one on, one at a time, to cause the change. Once you see how what is not working is influencing your life in a negative way, and you no longer want to live with it, you are then ready to shift it.

The next step calls for commitment. Sometimes it takes a long time to transform an area of your life that you wish to change, and it takes not giving up on it. I one time met a positive professor that much of the time looked on the bright side and rarely on the negative. I made a decision that I was going to be like him. This was difficult because other than him, I didn't have any positive role models. I had to look for inspiration in people I saw on *Oprah* and sometimes in Oprah herself, and gradually more and more positive people began showing up. I would notice the times when I wasn't being positive. I was only looking at the negative. I would then note that I still wasn't there yet. Then one day out of the blue, someone commented how positive I was, and I suddenly realized that I actually was positive and had made the shift. I couldn't have made that change if I hadn't been committed to being that.

The final step is to begin to believe that you can achieve metamorphosis, to see and challenge your thought processes that have led you to where you are now.

Journal activity: Make a list of what is working and not working in your life? Take on one of these areas and decide to transform it.

Challenging Our Thought Processes

Many of our beliefs that we have about the world and ourselves are not true. We developed some of these beliefs in childhood when we were too young to analyze and challenge what we knew about the world. As we grew older, those thought processes became more ingrained in us as we came across challenges in our lives that once again confirmed what we already believed about ourselves. To make our lives worse, we began to hide these beliefs inside ourselves, hoping that no one would notice them, and sometimes overcompensating for them to hide them deeper. The more we hid them, the deeper the roots took hold in our psyche. It takes significant shifts in our thinking to change some of these beliefs.

When I was a child, my mother would punish me when I would cry, so I began to feel that my emotions were wrong, and I needed to hide them. The more I thought that my feelings were wrong, the more I would hate myself when I showed them in front of others. I spent much time and energy not showing emotions in front of others. I would do much of what people asked me to do so that there would be no conflict where I might show my feelings. I married a man who validated the idea that my feelings were wrong. He saw my emotions as wrong and convinced me that I was crazy and needed help. I don't blame him, or my mother, for believing this because they each most likely had someone in their lives that convinced them that emotions were wrong.

It was my therapist who showed me that my emotions were normal. They weren't a sign of me being crazy. She was the one that helped me to accept my feelings as I was going through my divorce. When I cried, I knew that the crying was moving me one more step toward acknowledging my newfound situation. When I got angry and blew up, I knew it was another part of the process of being betrayed. Now I see my negative emotions as blessings that show me a wound that I need to heal. I created that thought because it empowers me instead of making me feel ashamed of my emotions.

To challenge your thought process, ask yourself when a thought is making you anxious, "Is that true?" Now, most of you probably can find an abundance of evidence to prove that the negative thoughts about yourself and others are true. The real challenge is to look for ways that prove your beliefs untrue. I couldn't believe that I was crazy when I had emotions. I had to ask myself if everyone who had emotions were crazy. I could see instances where it was beneficial to cry or to become angry about a misfortune. It was people who became angry about the state of the world that began to get involved and make changes.

The hard part is trying to find those negative beliefs about yourself that are running in the background of your life. I had a therapist that helped me with this one. Many of my other beliefs about myself have emerged over my lifetime. I still find that negative beliefs raise their ugly heads from time to time. I discover my negative beliefs whenever I take on some challenging project that makes me feel uncomfortable, and sure enough, my insecurities will emerge.

Journal activity: What are some negative thought processes that get in your way? What evidence can you find that they are not true?

Forgiveness

The first step to loving ourselves is forgiveness of our past shameful failures. We tend to punish ourselves for transgressions we have made that have hurt us or hurt others. We feel that carrying the guilt and punishing ourselves will compensate for the mistakes we made. When we continue to punish ourselves, we open ourselves up to punishment from others. What it does is take away from our soul what we need to be strong, healthy, and whole. Carrying around regret and shame will affect the people around us, as we don't trust ourselves or we lack the full joy we could have. We don't have to be perfect. We can make mistakes and recover from them. We can do that through the following steps:

Step 1: Look at where you have regrets or areas where you can't forgive yourself. An area where I had regret was missing my mother's funeral. I had wanted to be a part of it, and I asked my dad what I could do to help. He said that I could provide the music, and he picked out a song that he would like to hear. I downloaded a song that my mother used to play over and over when I was a child and that I thought would be appropriate. I took some time to think of some stories about my mother that I could tell at the funeral. I was fully prepared to make my mother's funeral exceptional.

Unfortunately, I did not plan for the weather that would hit that day. I had picked up my daughter and my grandson and was heading to my dad's small town in the mountains, which was two and a half hours away. I started up four hours before the funeral to have time to set up my speakers and my music. The traffic got worse and worse as we went, and at one point, the state closed the highway and was not letting anyone through. I called to let my dad know where I was and asked if he could postpone the funeral. Unfortunately, my dad said he couldn't. I finally got to the church a half hour after the funeral. Everyone who had attended had gotten there the night before. I regretted not coming up the night before as they had.

I began to look for more to punish myself for. I asked if the church had provided any music at the funeral, and when they hadn't, I felt awful. I asked if anyone had gotten up to speak, and once again I felt remorse that no one had gotten up in front to talk about her. I began blaming myself that it was because of me that my mother did not have the sendoff that she should have had. This was my daughters' first funeral as well, and they missed being able to say goodbye properly to their grandmother. I had a lot to feel guilty for, and I carried this guilt for quite a while.

Step 2: Look to see what effects your continuing regrets and guilt are having on you and the people around you. With my mother, I could see that my guilt and regrets were keeping me from being close to my dad. I felt I had let him down, and I felt weak as his oldest daughter. I felt that I couldn't be trusted with responsibilities and that he shouldn't rely on me for help. My regrets and guilt had propelled me back into being a victim. I tried blaming others for my lack of closure. I blamed my dad for having the funeral on such a bad day. I blamed the snow crews for not being able to keep the highway open because skiers were their biggest priority. I blamed my daughters for not being able to go the night before, although I had not asked them to take time off their jobs. I blamed my own job because I had felt that I couldn't take time off to leave a day early. It was blame, blame, blame. Considering that I hate dwelling too long in Victimville, I knew I had to correct this.

Step 3: Take responsibility for your mistake and ask yourself what you could have done differently. I knew I could have gone up a day early, and it was no one's fault except my own that I had missed my mother's funeral. I had to apologize to my family for not being there and not having the forethought to remember that sometimes the mountain passes close when there is inclement weather. I wrote my mother a letter asking for forgiveness and played the songs for her that I had downloaded. I told her in my letter the story that I had planned on telling at the funeral.

Asking forgiveness of others is sometimes easier than forgiving yourself. After apologizing to others, it is time to look at yourself and acknowledge your mistakes. Most of our mistakes were not mistakes that we meant to do. I did not intentionally miss my mother's funeral. I fully had intended to go. I, unfortunately, miscalculated the weather, and this was a human error. I realized that I probably would never do that again. I knew that if my dad ever needed me, I would do my best to not get stuck in that kind of a snowstorm again. I would definitely pre-plan.

After you forgive yourself, you do your best to make up for what you have done. One action that I take that I did not do before is to call my dad every week. I want him to know that he can count on me. I picked him up for a Thanksgiving dinner and made sure to arrive the day before so that if we couldn't get down from the mountains, he would not be spending his Thanksgiving alone.

Step 4: Say I forgive myself for....

Journal activity: Make a list of the mistakes you have made in your life that you still hold on to. By this, I mean mistakes that still cause you pain and shame to this day despite the fact that they happened many years ago. Say out loud to yourself that you forgive yourself for each mistake. Keep repeating this until you do feel the forgiveness. If these past events still have a charge for you after some real soul searching, find a trusted friend and read the list to them. Say out loud to them that you forgive yourself for each mistake on the list. Sometimes forgiveness doesn't happen when we are alone. If the transgression involves another person you have hurt, first forgive yourself for that and then write the other person a letter asking for forgiveness. If you can, reach out to that person and read your letter to him or her. This is not an easy endeavor to do; however, it will make a huge difference in how you then feel about yourself and that person.

Looking at Your Family of Origin

Much of who we are, came from our parents. We are either like them or polar opposite to them. Whether you want to be like them or not be like them, your parents are a huge part of how you operate in life and whom you choose as partners. Your parents were your role models at a critical stage of your development, and their influence was quite heavy on your makeup. If you don't take the time to look at your relationships with your parents and the events that shaped your views, you continue to let these events influence you unconsciously.

In my home, my mother was a huge influence on me because she was home most of the time and my dad was not. My mother cheated on my dad, we all knew about it, and it was a demon that tore our whole house apart. She once told me that I would probably cheat in my marriage because she had. I decided that whatever happened in my marriage, I was not going to do that.

Harville Hendrix opened up the idea that we will look for partners that resemble our caretakers. So although I didn't cheat in my marriage, I married a man who was like my mother. He cheated on me with people who made him feel special. It wasn't until after my divorce that I saw that I had married my mother. I wanted to avoid repeating that mistake, so I took on the task of healing my relationship with my her. Healing my relationship with my ex-husband would come later.

The first step in rebuilding my relationship was to forgive her. I became curious about who she was and how she had become the woman that I knew. Through talking to her about her upbringing in a household with a dismissive mother and an alcoholic father, I began to see her pain from childhood, and we began to heal our relationship. Not only were there things that I needed to forgive her for, but I also had events that I needed to apologize for. I had been vulgar and disrespectful to her at times and had justified it with her not being a good mom. I had to see that the problems I was having were not her fault. She had simply done the best she could with what she had.

If you are single and looking for your next relationship, take the time to get complete with the events that pained you from your childhood.

Journal activity: What painful memories do you have of your mother? What painful memories do you have of your father? How might these memories be influencing your life now? What can you forgive? What actions can you take with your mother or father to heal the past? What conversations could you have with them that would make a difference in your healing?

Creating Your Own Image

Many of you are harsh on who you are. So many people can't possibly look in the mirror without loathing. They don't look at themselves in the mirror anymore. You can't be that person in the mirror because that person is too short, tall, fat, skinny, or old. Yours is the body that you were given, and it's time that you love it. You need to accept who you are and how you got to where you are with your body. Maybe you have wrinkles from worrying, scars from tragedies, or stretch marks from having children. These are all part of the journey that you have been on in becoming who you are today. You are unique because of these experiences, and you alone can wear that body. You might as well wear it like an expensive outfit that you have given every cent to buy. There is probably someone out there that would kill to have your body, no matter how bad it looks to you. You are able to create the thoughts that you have concerning your body, and you might as well create positive ones as opposed to negative ones. There might be some characteristics that you can alter your appearance. Starting from a place of love for where you are right now will allow you to be patient with the changes and enjoy each step, rather than fighting the steps.

When you take on your appearance in the world, you begin a shift. Maybe you are someone who can't break out of old patterns and can't think in new and positive ways. Sometimes altering your appearance is what it takes to create an entirely new and confident you. Maybe you cut your hair if you have always had it long, perhaps you color it, maybe you find someone to give you a makeup lesson, or maybe you buy new clothes that are different from your old style. Whatever it takes to make you feel confident in who you are is what you need to take on.

I noticed that I had a pattern. When I was between relationships with men, I would work out, lose weight, and feel fantastic about myself. When I was in a relationship, I would become comfortable and let myself gain weight. Then I would be back to the same cycle as soon as the man was gone. What I finally got was that I needed to feel great about my own image at all times. This meant that I needed to make a radical change in my diet, exercise, and wardrobe. I was skilled at dieting for the short term. I was not skilled at creating healthy eating habits that lasted. When I finally understood that this body was all I had and I needed to take better care of it, I began shifting how I saw diet and exercise. This needed to be a lifetime change, not an "I will diet and exercise until I find a new guy or I fit into that outfit I bought." This was new for me because I was in a long-term relationship, and I was lucky that my partner chose to take on his health as well, especially when he did most the cooking. We began reading labels, shopping differently, and actually cooking. We got a gym membership and started riding bikes together. As I lost weight, I needed a new wardrobe. Instead of buying comfortable clothes and different colors of the same shirt, I had a mother-daughter team take me shopping. I let them dress me and tell me what they thought looked fabulous on me. I learned about fashion and having many different looks that felt great to wear. My confidence in my appearance grew, and as it grew, my confidence in other areas grew as well. People began noticing my changes at work and at home with my family.

Many nutritionists and fitness experts can help you with diet and exercise. On my own journey toward health, what made the most difference was a commitment toward being healthy. I needed to make this a lifelong commitment and not merely a short-term goal. I had to notice how I was growing healthier daily. I needed to get to genuinely know my body. I couldn't have done this if I had been fighting and loathing it. I had to become aware of what foods kept me up all night and what gave me bloating and stomach problems. I had to notice which foods made me crave foods that were unhealthy for me, and which ones gave me energy. I had to see how my body was responding to the exercise. At first, I was out of breath and sometimes panicked at not being able to breathe. I had to begin to notice when I could go longer without being completely out of breath. I thanked my body after each workout, no matter how short the workout was or hard it was. This was my way of loving my body and being patient with the process.

Journal activity: What have you been saying about your body that doesn't serve your best interest? What is pleasing about your body that would make someone else want to have it? What health and nutrition goals could you set to take care of your body? Who can you talk to that could help you with your goals?

Created Context of Others

Creating the Frog

You might be in a relationship that you have begun to see as a mistake. You might have seen your partner as the "one" at one time, and now all you see are faults. The personality traits that you once loved, are now irritations. You might have loved your partner's ambition at one time, except now you are irritated that your partner spends all his or her time at work trying to climb to the top and less time with you. You might have loved how mysterious he was, except now you see him as uncommunicative and closed up. You might have loved your partner's young spirit and found it delightful to be around, except now you hate that your partner wants to play much of the time and doesn't seem to want to grow up. You are now creating that person as a frog and no longer see the prince or goddess.

Rousing the troops

When we begin to have irritation and resentment for a person, we start to look for faults. We overlook the right actions and tend to notice the wrong ones. To justify our thinking, we find others to agree with us about this person. These others that agree with us become our troops. These troops start to see that one side of the person that is your view, and they begin to hold the same opinion. They will react differently to your significant other and notice his or her faults as well. They will ask you why you put up with this or that and why you don't leave that relationship. The more your friends agree with you, the more you begin to believe that your relationship is doomed and broken. In fact, you cause such agreement in them about your partner's faults that even when you are happy and feeling connected with your partner, your troops will point out those errors again and remind you that this is temporary and that your partner will let you down again.

When you talk poorly about anyone with friends or family, including complaining, and try to have them take your side in a matter, it is gossip. You might have had the impression that gossip is spreading rumors about people that are not true, and what you are saying about this person is not gossip because it's true. You have to realize that it is solely correct from your perspective, and thus it is a lie. We believe our views, and when we doubt our perspectives at all, we tell others our stories and convince them to come to our point of view. This often happens in the workplace when you are frustrated with someone, and you begin to go to coworkers, to complain about that person. Pretty soon there is a big clique of individuals that do not like a person in the workplace, and it spreads a lot of negativity. I have been on the side where I have turned against my boss with a bunch of people and felt like we were all fighters for right in a situation. I remember that I took part in this, but now I don't remember what the issue was. I remember my boss walking in on a group of us meeting and complaining about her and how uncomfortable the situation was. I regretted it immediately.

At that same job, I was to severely receive the lesson of gossip like no other. There was a new woman who started at the detention facility where I worked. She was creative and loving, and for some reason, I hated her. She shared an office with me, and we were so different. Where I was disorganized and had my piles, she had her paperwork neatly filed away. I had my students' work taped to the wall to inspire me daily. She saw this as messy and not attractive to look at. One weekend, she came in and painted and wallpapered the whole office. It was a rose in the heather because we worked at a juvenile jail where there was no beauty. I should have been grateful to have this peaceful place to come back to during my breaks from the students. I wasn't. I was angry because she had moved all my stuff around; I felt it was an attack on me and how I organized. I began telling people, from coworkers to friends and some of our students, my complaints about this woman. Not surprisingly, it got back to her. I got called into the office, and there she sat with tears in her eyes. I had never felt as ashamed of myself as I did then. After she had told me what she had heard from our students, I apologized profusely. She then left, and I got a real scolding from my supervisor. This supervisor had been through some outside training, and he showed me that my negativity toward this woman had stemmed from my own lack of self-worth and doubts about myself that I was projecting onto her. I left that office with a lot of soul searching to do.

Our troops can be supportive and can help us through some difficult times, but we need to be aware of what kind of support we are seeking from them and what kind of information we are feeding to them. If they are encouraging us to resolve our issues with people, they are beneficial to our relationships. If they are only agreeing with us and badmouthing the people we struggle with, this is not beneficial and can be more harmful.

Journal activity: What messages do you find yourself saying to your friends and family about the people in your life? Are they positive or negative messages?

Should Be ...

Much of the pain that we have in our relationships with our children, lovers, bosses, or selves comes from this idea of who people should be. We have formed these opinions over the course of our lives as we watched television or read books about these ultimate role models that were not real. Many of the shows that we watched on television had characters that were perfect mothers, fathers, friends, or lovers. Girls grew up with stories of princes that loved them and would fight dragons for them. Boys saw mothers and wives that did all the cooking, cleaning, and caring for the children. This was the type of programming that I saw as a child. Today, we have reality television that influences our society. The roles that we see today are of people who are privileged and don't have jobs; they party a lot and are aggressive with each other. The cameras love to exploit the gossiping and the fights amongst people. The millennials today believe that they don't need jobs, and they don't need driver's licenses. They believe that it is okay to purely live at home and be taken care of by their parents. We wonder where they learn these ideas.

I grew up watching shows like *The Brady Bunch, Leave It to Beaver,* and *The Andy Griffith Show.* I had a belief that mothers "should be" compassionate and loving as well as wise and give great advice. They "should be" able to cook and clean the house. My mother was not that, and thus there was a barrier with my mother. I had the wrong mother. It didn't matter that she was only sixteen when she had me and had never had the chance to grow up and be independent. She was the wrong mother. When a man that I was connecting with and wanting to date once mentioned that my daughters chose me, I thought that was outrageous because there was no way that I had chosen my mother. She was the wrong mother. He explained his belief about how we come into life with a purpose, and we choose the parents that are going to build our character to fulfill that purpose. I later saw that my mother was the perfect mother to create the person that I needed to be to be a loving mother, writer, and a relationship coach. Her rejection of me as a child, helped me to be independent, to love reading (which was my escape), and to love writing (which was my way to could express my feelings openly without punishment).

We form beliefs about how someone "should be" from our families of origin. If our father valued his job above all else and took a lot of criticism from his boss, then we should have a tough skin and take criticism from our bosses. Our partners had better be able to stand criticism from their bosses as well. When they quit a job during a poor evaluation, suddenly we look down at them and doubt that they have the character that we are looking for in a person. We can't accept that maybe they were asserting themselves and refusing to stay in a job that brings down their spirit and self-worth.

My dad was the kind of man who would put up with anything at his job. I do value my jobs and have put up with a lot of criticism in them because I thought that was what it took to support my family. These were his values, and this is how I felt people "should be." I no longer judge people who have quit their jobs. Nor do I judge myself for wanting to leave a job where I am not valued. I look at whenever I use the word *should,* either for myself or for others, and realize that it actually causes me heartache when I hold people to certain standards, and they are not meeting them.

Journal activity: Look at the "should be" dialogue that you say to yourself about the people in your life. How did you come to have these views about people?

Creating the Prince or Goddess

Creating "frogs" is a cycle that is hard to break, and there are opinions that you hold about people that you know are true. This is now a lens that you view your relationship through, and it clouds all that is happening in your relationship. It's like the ski goggles that you put on that make the terrain yellow at first. Eventually, you adapt to them, and you no longer see the yellow. The great news is that you can shift that lens and begin to see that person as a prince, goddess, angel, or teacher. You have the ability to create who the other person is, and he or she doesn't actually have to change at all. Let's face it, no one is perfect, and the other person is probably seeing the frog side of you as well. What you can do is begin to tell yourself that this is the ideal person that you need in your life to teach you what you are missing, and the negative traits you see are your perceptions and not that person's. Suddenly, you will begin to notice the benefits of having him or her around.

Accepting Others

I once heard the definition that love is accepting others for who they are, and for who they are not. This is that unconditional love that each of us yearns for from the depths of our souls. We had that at birth, and we want that to return. No one expects infants to be or act a certain way when they are born. We just respond to their needs and care for them. Many people's spiritual belief revolves around a higher power that accepts them for all their faults and loves them despite the mistakes they have made.

Who are we to go around judging others as right or wrong when we probably have the same faults as them? In fact, the bona fide flaws that irritate us in others are what we are repeatedly struggling within ourselves. If we are truly going to unconditionally love others, we have to love all their faults as well as their positive qualities.

I remember the touching scene in *Good Will Hunting* where the psychologist Sean, played by Robin Williams, explains to Will that he remembers that when his wife would sleep, she would fart. He told this story proudly and said that these were the idiosyncrasies about his wife that he recalled and missed the most. I thought that was an emotional scene because it showed how much he accepted his wife for who she was and had not expected her to be perfect.

You might be wondering how you welcome others' faults when you see that their flaws are hurting them and not serving them. You might want to fix them, and you might also want to buy them this book so that they can be fixed. Accepting them does not mean that you think what they are doing is right. A parent who has a child that is addicted to drugs does not decide that the drugs are acceptable. The parent can accept that the child is on his or her own journey in this life and is learning and teaching others the lessons that need to be drawn in this lifetime. The hero in the hero's journey must descend into hell and confront the devil to learn what is virtuous and to become resilient. The addict might need to hit bottom before being able to see that he or she is an addict and can't live life like that one more day. For a parent, this is excruciating because there is the fear that the child might die before coming out of this. We all should stand in the possibility that there will be a brighter, glorious future for our children and not live our lives believing they will die. This is not a belief that serves you or them. You need to love and accept them and yet hate the addiction. This does not mean you don't help them in healthy ways when they ask for it. Wait for them to ask for it, and then decide whether you are truly helping or just enabling them.

Recognizing Their Commitments

When you begin to accept others for who they are, you will notice the commitments that they are committed to. All actions and arguments have a commitment behind them, and it is our job to look at what the action or argument is actually trying to communicate. Let's say that your partner nags you about your socks that you leave in the bathroom, and it no longer becomes about how much they hate you. It becomes how committed they are for the both of you to live in a beautiful environment. Another example is when someone blows up at you for spending too much money; they are passionately committed to both people's security.

As a school teacher of students with emotional disabilities, I had to look for behaviors and ask myself what the children wanted that made them exhibit this behavior. These were usually needs of belonging, attention, power, or avoidance of a task. Both children and adults alike do not know how to ask for what they need and instead have developed ways to have their needs met. When I saw what the child needed, I tried to provide him or her with the desired want in a productive way. An example of this would be, if a child seemed to talk over me a lot and I determined that he or she needed my attention, I might stand closer to that child and give him or her more attention. I might include that child's name in examples or scenarios that I would give to the class. Giving students what they needed in class helped me to have better classroom control and allowed me to have a better relationship with my students.

We sometimes fight back when we feel that we are being controlled, manipulated, or made to act in some way that we don't want to. There is a rebel in all us that refuses to go along with the expectation of others. This rebellion doesn't serve us when it comes to relationships. The rebel doesn't see what other people want or are committed to. The rebel doesn't see the love and concern that a person might have. I have suffered myself from this rebellious spirit.

When I was co-teaching with four different teachers, one teacher called a meeting together with the other three educators and proceeded to propose some alternate schedules for my time. The rebel began to bubble up in me. I was not going to let someone dictate my schedule to me. I thought I knew what was best for my students and me that I serviced and that no one should tell me otherwise. It blew up into a huge argument, and the teacher threw me out of her room with some choice obscenities. I left the room feeling that I had won the argument because I had not let her gain control over me and I had not stooped so low as to scream obscenities. What I didn't see was her frustration with some of the kids who were struggling in her class and her commitment to having me in the room helping them with these struggles. I also didn't recognize her trust that I was an answer to this problem. She and I both had the same passion for helping the children but disagreed on the solution. I can admit that I was wrong and have since made it a point to clean things up with her and see her commitment.

Journal activity: Write some actions that irritate you. What do you think the person who is doing the actions is seriously committed to? How have you stood in the way of that person having what he or she needs or wants? What actions can you commit to that will create a better relationship?

Time to Clean House

So now that you see how you have been hurting people in your life, making them the bad guys and believing they should be another way, what do you do now? It's somewhat like the ninth step of AA, in which you need to make amends with people. It's time to admit how you have been the jerk in the relationship and have been the reason why the relationship is not working. This is painful to do because we don't like admitting that we have made mistakes, and we hope that we can be better around the person and not have to admit our mistakes. This is a vital step in creating relationships because you might have hurt other people, and they may be holding on to that pain. Admitting mistakes keeps you from continuing to make the mistakes again. This is a way to shatter that lens that we have for others and see them for who they truly are. Many times, when you admit that you have been a jerk, you are not surprising the person that you are confessing to.

They know that you have been stand-offish and not genuine with them. The benefits of cleaning messes up are that you begin to love people—not only the person you are cleaning up with but all people. You begin to experience love from them.

I knew a woman who was having all sorts of problems with her mother-in-law. She had gotten to the point where she refused to be in the same room as the woman and would leave the house when the mother-in-law came to see her husband and the kids. She had all kinds of stories about how the woman was unaccepting of her, judgmental, and not supportive of her marriage. When she saw that she had created these judgments about her mother-in-law, she understood that she was being no better than the person that she saw judging her. She realized that she could be the one to heal this relationship and finally called her and talked to her about it. She found that the mother-in-law was hurt because her daughter-in-law didn't like her. She saw that the mother-in-law was committed to her son's happiness, and since the woman was committed to her husband's happiness as well, they actually shared a commitment. After this conversation, she was no longer dreading visits from her mother-in-law. She was welcoming her, and the two women became friends.

You might be thinking of your mother-in-law or someone else and thinking, "Yeah, that was nice for her, but you don't know my mother-in-law, sister, husband ... fill in the blank. They are ... fill in the blank." Here is where you have to challenge yourself to realize that there is a significant probability that this is not true. When you begin to see that there is any possibility that it is not true, it is your responsibility to clean it up. The more you do this, the easier it becomes. The first person you talk to is, much of the time, the hardest one.

Journal activity: List the people in your life that you are making wrong for some reason, or that you are withholding love from, or that you are avoiding or not being loving toward in some ways. Start with the easiest one and either call or set up a date to see that person. If it's your spouse or your children, find some time to sit down with them and talk to them about the regrets you have about your mistakes and the effects on the relationship. If there is an issue you are holding a grudge over, admit it and forgive them.

Becoming Their Greatest Fan

Now that you are beginning to recognize the excellent qualities in others, it is time to become their greatest fan. It is time to show appreciation for these qualities that you are beginning to see as beneficial. Maybe you feel your husband acts like a child, except you notice that he likes to play with the kids, and the children light up when he comes home. You can start recognizing him for his role as a dad. You might mention what a marvelous provider he is and how he works hard to support you and the children. Suddenly, instead of being the child in the relationship, he gets to feel like a man, and what's more, the more you recognize him as a man, the more man he becomes. Mother Teresa once said, "Kind words are simple, but their echoes are endless."

Nobody likes empty praise, so look for positive behaviors that are genuine, that you indeed appreciate him doing. Especially if he isn't someone who wants praise, do it anyway. Eventually, he will feel that he deserves it. Tell him that you love him, and give him the attention he deserves. Be present when he talks and listen for the gold in him, and you will begin to see it.

Repair starts with your friends and family because you have now tainted their view of some people. You need to exclusively communicate positive aspects about your partner to them and admit that your complaints were putting distance between the two of you and not benefiting the relationship. Explain how committed you are to the relationship and ask for them to support you in this. Be an inspiration to the people in your life, and see if they can follow your lead with the relationships in their lives. If you notice that you are surrounded by negative people whose sole purpose is to put others down and gossip, it might be time to distance yourself from the negativity. Don't start judging them and wanting to change them. Merely love them from afar, and remember that you were once a part of the group and gossiping as well.

Creating Memories

Many times, after years of resignation and struggle with a partner, you begin to have the belief that you don't have any pleasant memories, but if you dig deep, you can find some. You can share them with your partner. If you acknowledge the creative plans your partner has devised in the past that have given you joy, your partner not only knows that those ideas have given you pleasure, but he or she might now have a clue as to what it was that made you happy. Your partner might not have felt acknowledged at the time for these efforts and felt you didn't value him or her. When you share these memories, you need to share them as an acknowledgement to your partner and not as a "You used to do ... and now you don't."

It is important for a couple to take on making new delightful memories. When your concerns are solely on what new and exciting memories you can create and no longer about the clutter in the house, the rest begins to go away, and you begin to ignite your passion toward one another. This could be a time that you take on doing those activities that you have wanted to do together but maybe didn't have the time or the money for. Over the years, you might have buried those dreams and goals because you felt like they were not going to ever come to fruition.

If it seems difficult to come up with ideas for creating memories, think back to some of the memories that you are fond of. What were you doing? What made them so special? You can begin to create romance out of any memories you want, simply by believing them to be romantic. I recently was helping my daughter out of a difficult situation, which took time away from my partner—time that I had promised I would not touch because we were working opposite shifts. I called him and let him know what was going on, believing that he was going to think that I was once again enabling my daughter and not empowering her to solve her problems on her own. Instead, I found him to be supportive, and as I finally drove home to him, I began thinking of how supportive of me he was and what a fantastic man I had in my life. I was thinking of ways to repay him, and then I walked in to find a beautiful bouquet of flowers. This became one of my most romantic memories, and I know that I'm the one who is able to create it as a romantic story. After all, most romantic stories are just an event until you take the time to think about them as romantic and to tell them to others. You can create any event as romantic.

A recent story I have is about when the two of us were out shopping for some appropriate clothes to wear on our trip to Paris. I tried on clothing such as trench coats and leather jackets, which I don't usually wear, for him. He tried on leather jackets and sweaters that I picked out. I let him influence what he liked seeing me in, and I also got him to buy a couple of sweaters (he didn't own a single sweater until that day). It was a pleasant day, and we were connecting. We were living into a future of Paris and the adventures we were going to have there. This was romantic in all senses or not romantic at all, depending on how you look at it. I chose to look at it as a scene out of a romantic comedy instead of a standard event of a shopping trip. So the next time you are going on a casual outing with your partner, look to see how you can create it as a romantic adventure.

Created Sex

If you bought this book to work on relationships with your children, your co-workers, or some other family member, you might want to skip this chapter. If you want to not only have a better relationship with your lover but also experience better sex, read on.

You might be asking yourself why you should create sex. You might feel that sex should be spontaneous and be whatever it is, but let's face it, sex that is not created can be less satisfying, non-existent, or not what you wanted at the time. Many of your ideas about sex were designed when you were in your twenties, and you were much younger. You are older now and still comparing your sex life to when you were younger, more energetic, and more limber, with more stamina.

Many people have sex not because they want it or need it, but because someone else seems to want it or need it more. This sex is not satisfying on the deepest levels for either person. The person who doesn't want sex might be wishing to be elsewhere, or to be doing something else. That person then resents the person who needs the sex. The person receiving the sex gets to have sex but doesn't have the real connection of the partner that is giving in to his or her needs. That person feels rejected on some levels.

To create sex allows you to have the sex life that you want and need that is satisfying and deeply connecting to the other person.

Preparing for Sex

For some couples, sex needs to be scheduled or planned. Let's face it, if we waited till we both felt like having sex, we could be waiting a long time. Many of us lead busy lives, and we are tired much of the time. Back when you and your partner were new, you had chemical hormones firing off that made you want to have sex all the time. Now you look back at that and say to yourself, "Those were the days," and you might be waiting till the children are out of the house, and then later for retirement, and it becomes harder and harder to initiate sex.

Scheduling sex does not have to take away the intimacy of it. In fact, scheduling can make it an exciting experience that you are looking forward to. You now have a day and time in your future that you can work yourself into. You can make sure you look sexy, shave those hairy parts, and maybe buy some massage oil for the date. It can go along with a dinner or other romance. You can send suggestive texts to each other and flirt throughout the day or week. This can all be part of the foreplay leading up to sex.

Some couples might negotiate how much sex to have, when they will have it, and who is going to initiate it. You can decide which days or nights you will have quickie sex and when you are going to have gourmet sex that is longer and more satisfying.

Preparing for sex is a time for clearing out all your worries that could be on your mind before you are ready to have sex. If the electric bill hasn't been paid and you are afraid that the lights could be turned off at any moment, you should make this a priority. If the children need to be fed so that they are not banging on the door, you need to do this as well. Women many times need to be relaxed before having sex, and setting the mood or having a bubble bath beforehand can be helpful.

This time before sex is an excellent time to remove any resentment that you might be holding onto about your partner. When the experts say, "Don't ever go to bed angry," this definitely applies to sex. If you are frustrated with the other person, you might need to iron out your issues before the two of you can have sex. Forgiveness needs to happen. Sex on top of resentment can hurt the relationship further. So take the time to communicate what you have been resenting the person for before having sex.

Journal activity: How often do you want to have sex and how often does your partner? What are some dates in the future that you would like to reserve as sex dates? What are some chores you need to do to get ready for sex? What do you consider as foreplay that gets you going for sex? What does your partner consider as foreplay?

Present during Sex

Being present during sex is crucial for both partners. You will not feel satisfied if you are thinking about the laundry that needs to be folded or the bills that need to be paid. It's like meditation; when you find your mind wandering, bring it back to the moment and what you are doing at the time. You are able to create your thoughts. You could be thinking about how much you love that person or have memories of the first time the other person ever touched you, or about how marvelous it feels.

People want to feel desired. When you touch the other person, either in the bedroom or out of the bedroom, try to convey through your touch how much love you feel for that person and how exquisite you want it to feel for him or her. This needs to be a selfless act that you don't expect to be reciprocated. When you touch that person with presence and love, for his or her pure enjoyment, your partner can feel it as that. When you touch someone, to have that person to take out the trash or to have sex with you, the person feels manipulated to some respect.

Setting intentions before sex can be a way of creating great sex. Maybe you set the intention that you are going to simply have a grand time, and whether you climax or not is not as important. Maybe your intention is that your partner feels love, connection, and intimacy. Maybe your intention is to go slow and have your partner passionately feel desired. Having positive intentions before having sex can keep your mind from going to negative places or away from what is happening at the time.

As you are able to set your intentions for the sexual encounter, you are able to create who your partner is for you. You can create your partner as confident and capable of giving you great sex, and your partner will feel that you trust him or her to actually do this. If you go into the encounter doubting your partner's ability to please you, your partner will pick up on this and will have trouble performing.

Fear does not belong in the bedroom. When you are afraid of your body and how it will respond to sex, you are not entirely present. You need to love your body first. You need to love the experience and not have expectations for it. If you have expectations that the other person will have the best orgasm of his or her life, you are setting yourself up for a possible letdown because you are not responsible for the other person's orgasm; the other person is. That doesn't mean that you solely take what you need and don't give selflessly to the partner. It does mean that you don't think about the other person the whole time and have fears of whether it is good or bad for that person. That puts an expectation on the sex. "In order to have an orgasm, I must or he must ..." This doesn't allow for some passionately great feelings to come up and to intensely experience your own pleasure.

Communication for Sex

Communication is the key for a couple to experience great sex. You can't expect your partner to know what you like and don't like in bed. Your partner might be going off what someone else liked, what someone recommended in a magazine, or what you pretended to like last time when you faked your orgasm. Don't ever fake your orgasm. Not only is this inauthentic and deceitful, but it will give the other person a false sense of what you like and don't like.

You might be thinking that there is no way that you can communicate about sex with your lover; yet you have to be able to do this if you want to create great sex. Some people can talk about sex together through watching porn or reading a book about sex. They can say what they would like to try or what they don't like. You can discuss sexual ideas at a time when you are not planning to have sex soon. This can be done in a non-threatening way without pressures or criticism. Talking about sex can be vulnerable for people, although it can create intimacy. It is important not to make another person feel wrong for his or her ideas or inadequacies for sex. If you do, it could kill the security between a couple. People need to be confident in bed. Criticizing someone will take away that security that the person needs.

Communication during sex could be a gentle guiding of a hand to the right place or a moaning when your partner has hit that spot that sends shivers through your body. A full sentence of "I love you," "You're beautiful," or "You really turn me on" is a great way of communicating to your partner that he or she is desired.

Created Meanings of Sex

Many people believe that sex has its own intrinsic meanings. If you have sex too soon, the other person won't respect you. If you have too many partners, you are a whore. If that person loved you, he or she would have sex with you. If that person were attracted to you, he or she would have intercourse you. Sex is only meant for reproducing. Sex is dirty or a sin. Sex makes people behave in ways that they don't want to behave. These are not intrinsic meanings of sex. They are made-up meanings that humans created. Animals do not have such beliefs about sex. They purely have it. Sex has no meaning at all except for the meanings we give it, and many times, we make up meanings of sex that don't allow us to enjoy it thoroughly.

If you have a belief that sex is only meant for reproduction, and you don't want children, you are probably not going to have much sex. If you think that sex should be reserved for the person you are going to spend the rest of your life with, and you made the mistake of having it with the boy you went out with last night, you are going to carry around a lot of shame and guilt about this. If you have a belief that a woman must have an orgasm every time she has sex with you, and she doesn't, you might feel like a failure and begin to doubt your abilities in bed. If you believe a man will have an erection every time naturally if he is attracted to you, then the first time that he has trouble with the erection, you will make this mean that he is no longer attracted to you. To be able to have a sex life that is created and not limited, you should give up all these limiting beliefs. You should begin to create meanings that are empowering and destroy the ones that are disempowering.

To create meanings in sex that knock your socks off in bed, you need to let go of the old beliefs and begin to use your creativity. I'm not saying that you need to go out and start swinging with another couple or buy handcuffs and blindfolds, unless you both find it intriguing. What I mean about creating new meanings is you can take any scenario around love making and give it power, love, romance, or devotion. To do this, you need to let go of your past experiences and the meanings that you gave them. Let's say you were great in bed in your twenties and were able to last half the night, and you would like to be able to do that again. Now you can say that you are great in your forties, and you only last as long as your partner needs you to last, which is better for the both of you. Let's say that in the past, you could merely look at each other, and you were falling into bed together, but now with kids, you need to schedule sex. You can make up how much better the two of you are in bed together now that you are parents and partners. You might have a belief that sex was so much better when you first started having it. In reality, the two of you knew little about each other. You were more worried about repulsing, hurting, or offending your partner. Lust hormones drove your sex life, as opposed to the sex you have now. Now you are more comfortable with each other, you each know what the other likes, and you have developed real love and understanding for each other.

So how do you create these empowering meanings around sex? First, you begin to look at the invalidating thoughts that you are having now about your sexual experiences. What meanings have you given to sex that make you not want to have it? I had a lover that was no longer initiating sex with me, and I began to make this mean that he was no longer attracted to me. When I finally got the courage to talk to him about it, he said that he was struggling with achieving erections. I asked if he had been to see a doctor, and he said the doctor told him that he needed to give up smoking, drinking, and eating bad foods. I then made it mean that he valued his bad habits over having sex with me, and this did not help our sex life. I finally had to give up the belief that the man should always initiate the sex if he were attracted to me. My sex life improved dramatically. I looked for other proof that I was still attractive to him and no longer looked for it in the bedroom. Whether I initiated it or he initiated it meant nothing. What it meant was that we were having sex again and were closer than before, when I was not feeling his attraction, and he was feeling like a failure.

Creating new meanings around sex can allow you to open up to some of the ideas that your partner would like to try in the bedroom. If you have carried around meanings such as "This or that is too kinky or abnormal," you have not been willing to try those experiences. This might be some fantasy that your partner enjoys, but has never had the chance to experience with you. There are fantasies that you might think are too painful or too degrading that you still are opposed to, and probably should be opposed to; however, this does open a few more doors that were not open before.

Journal activity: Look at all your beliefs that you have about sex. Some of these might have originated from your parents and some from friends or your faith. Ask yourself which beliefs are holding you back from having a great sex life. Which ones could you give up? Which ones could you transform into powerful beliefs that work for you instead?

Creating What Is Sexy

We, unfortunately, let magazines and television create what is sexy. These images aren't real. What is real are the people you experience around you that have not been touched up, had plastic surgery, or starved themselves silly. When we hold ourselves or our partners to these kinds of standards, we are clearly let down because no one can reach that perfection. When you hold yourself to standards of when you were thirty years younger, you can never feel sexy in your older age. Not feeling sexy in the bedroom can make you feel anxious or self-conscious about having sex. It keeps you from being present.

Many of us are ashamed to call ourselves sexy; however, it is time that we begin to create what is sexy in life. We have the ability to define sexy in our own terms and make sure those conditions include ourselves and our partners. One time at a meditation retreat at the Chopra Center, we were asked to say who we were. We started with "I am ..." and we finished it with whatever came to mind. I was in a large circle with men and women and was near the end. When it came around to me, one of the "I ams" I blurted out that no one else had said was "I am sexy." I had been using this to describe myself for months, despite the fact that I was two years from reaching fifty, and I had lines on my face and some weight around my middle. I knew that saying that I was sexy made me feel sexy, and it was benefiting my self-confidence, my weight loss goals, and my relationship itself. My partner was used to hearing me talk about how sexy I was and also agreed with me most of the time. (That's how you know you have an exceptional partner.) What I hadn't ever done was say it in a group that might not deem me sexy by their standards. When I blurted this out to my group, there was somewhat of a small gasp in the group, and the meaning that I make of this is that many people there were wishing that they had either said this or had the guts to say this in a group of strangers. There might have been some who were sizing me up as sexy or not sexy; however, that doesn't matter to me.

So what can you now add to your definition of what is sexy? Maybe it's a guy who recently read a book to your child. Maybe it is a woman who had dinner ready for you when you got home. Maybe it's a guy that loves to have sex with the lights on because he loves to look at you. Whatever you create as the definition, you can feel delighted that you are included in this private club that only you and your partner share, and can exclude the supermodels of the day.

Created Partnerships

Why

Many of us have reached our independence in different ways, and we like our independence. We find it difficult to ask for help from others, and we sometimes would rather rely on ourselves than have a partner, who will have different opinions and a different way of management. We have beliefs that partnership takes work, and it can be sometimes stressful if we don't live up to other people's expectations, or they don't pull their own weight in the partnership. Why can't we simply go it and do it alone?

These beliefs might be true, except that we all long for partnership on our deepest levels. We want someone that will be there to help us carry the burden. We want someone that will bring qualities to projects that we are lacking. We want someone to help us work through problems and sometimes take over when we have no clue what we are doing.

Another reason that we can benefit from partnerships is that when we have people that believe in us and believe in what we can accomplish, we no longer get to skate through life. We begin to accomplish goals we thought we were unable to achieve. The great people in life, such as Abraham Lincoln, Thomas Edison, and many others, were not alone making decisions. They had partners and sometimes teams of people that believed in them and what they were doing. They created these teams through being people that others wanted to know and help.

Whether you want a partner to help raise your children, someone to help you open a business or merely someone that you can bounce ideas off of, you need to create this kind of partnership. You need a partnership that you can trust. You need one that will be strong and one that you can depend on when the going becomes rough with whatever you are doing.

What's the Project?

So what is it that you would like to take on in life that you feel you want to accomplish? What is it that you need help with? Knowing what you want is an excellent first step toward knowing what qualities you are looking for in a partner. If you don't know the qualities that you are looking for, you won't know who to ask to be that partner.

Years ago, I longed to have a partner to help me raise my daughters. I wanted to have someone that I could rely on to come and help me if my car or a gadget broke down that I didn't know how to fix. I was looking for someone who had a job so that I could feel financially secure. I basically needed someone that was reliable, handy, and excellent with kids and had a job.

With the book I'm writing, I need people to believe in me as a writer. I need people to read it and give me feedback. I am mainly looking for partners that will be honest with me and not solely tell me what I want to hear. I'm looking for people who read relationship books and are willing to read mine and give me feedback.

I coached a young man who had very altruistic goals of helping the homeless. He was in many bands, and he wanted to put on a concert to raise money for his cause. He was looking for partners that knew the right actions to take and whom to ask favors of. He needed people who knew what the homeless people in his community needed. He needed partners that could donate supplies to his cause.

Journal activity: What are some of the goals you have not accomplished and still see as rewarding? What would help to motivate you on these goals? What could others assist you with?

Knowing Your Strengths and What You Need

To be able to pick the right partners, you need to know what you are looking for. If you know your strengths at what you do best, it is beneficial to know what you sometimes struggle with so that you can find partners that have that ability. It's somewhat like playing a role-playing video game where you have built up a team of a thief, a warrior, a wizard, and an archer. When you have a team of players where each has a strength that the others lack, there is balance. Maybe you are strong with action and lack organization, and someone else can provide that. Perhaps you are thoughtful and lack the ability to make decisions when they need to be made. This is where you can turn to someone else on your team and know that he or she has this, and you trust this person to take on that part. If you take on partners but continue to do the entire project yourself, you might never have the experience of partnering with people and seeing their full potential. You might not also see the full potential of the project.

I once took on a project at my school to raise food for families of my students that needed it. For a long time, it stayed in the back of my mind, and I had no clue how to make it happen. I finally e-mailed the school with my idea and held my first meeting. Only four showed up; however, they were the most powerful partners that I could have had. I lacked the ability to ask for what I needed, so unless I was going to provide fifty families with food myself, I needed someone who didn't mind asking for others for help. One of the teachers stated that she was skilled at bugging people and influencing them to help out the families. I had another woman who knew people that donated from her church, and we got more supplies. Before I knew it, we had fifty boxes of food for Thanksgiving and fifty for Christmas as well. After asking for help, I found that the project was not hard at all. I only had to organize the meetings.

Current Partners

You might already have partners in your life right now, except you don't see them as partners. They might be right in front of you, and you take them for granted as casual acquaintances. They might be people who admire you or look up to you. You need to look at your current relationships and ask yourself whether any of them would be an acceptable fit for whatever project you are taking on. You might already have someone in your life who wanted to marry you, and you never saw that person in that way before. You need to open yourself up to the possibilities that exist with the current people in your life.

Sometimes, partners can come from the most unlikely places. I was a single mother, and I wanted more than anything for someone to share the parenting of my children. When they got older and sometimes more challenging, I knew I needed help. I had not been inclined to find a suitable man to take this on, so eventually, I looked to the one man that had been there all the time, although I hadn't been letting him be a parent to my children. That was my daughters' dad, my ex-husband. I had so many reasons not to want him to take a part in their parenting because of my own issues with him; however, he was all I had.

On the downside, you might have partners that are not the right ones for the project that are keeping you from achieving what you wish to achieve. They might be negative, putting your ideas down and telling you that there is no way you will ever accomplish your dreams. These people might not be carrying their weight in a project; for example, they might be living in your home and not looking for a job.

It might be time to assess your current relationships with what you are committed to doing and having in your life. Begin to see whether you can build a team with what you have or whether you need to look elsewhere for people that embrace your visions.

Journal activity: Write a list of individuals that you have in your life and put their qualities down next to their names. Decide which of these people have the qualities you need to help you go forward and accomplish what you wish to achieve.

Recruiting Partners

Now that you have a few ideas of people who could support you in your project, it is time to think about asking them to be your partners. Before you talk to them, you need to think of how they can mutually benefit from a partnership with you. You need to think about what you bring to the table that can show them that they want to be in partnership with you. What qualities do you possess that they can find as an asset in what they want to accomplish? It is always important to think about what they want to achieve in their lives. Maybe you are thinking about opening a business and want someone to help you run it; you need to think about what you know that person possesses that makes you confident that he or she can do the job. You need to know what the other person can receive out of helping you run your business.

When you first talk to the person, start by acknowledging him or her for an accomplishment that is noteworthy. You then need to present your idea as an opportunity for the person and then last, but not least, ask him or her to be part of the project.

When I realized that I needed my daughters' father to partner with me to raise our children, I knew I had to come clean and admit that I hadn't allowed him to do that. I had to admit that every time the girls had problems with him, I would swoop in and rescue the girls without allowing him to work through his problems with them. I had to apologize for this and let him know that I was now going to trust him with this and partner with him so that the girls could no longer play us against each other. I had to support his discipline of them, just as I needed him to support my discipline of them. This was not easy because I saw him as harsh and abusive; but I knew that what I was doing was not working with them either.

Creating the Current Partnership

To have a successful partnership, you need to believe two concepts. One is that the person that you are in partnership with is doing the best he or she can with what he or she has to work with. The second is that you need to want the other to succeed more than yourself.

Believing that someone is doing the best he or she can with what he or she has got is not always easy. We tend to think that people should have the same values and competency as ourselves, and we tend to dismiss them as if we feel they are beneath us.

Being a teacher for many years, I have heard teachers badmouth the parents that they work with. Those same teachers have trouble working with parents and creating partnerships with them.

Working in the field of special education, I have had to have many a meeting with parents. This can be an intensely delicate subject because many parents of special needs children are adversarial, and they know their rights. Many of them are quick to point fingers at the teachers that work with their children. I was a teacher that didn't know how to relate to parents. I was afraid of them for a while and let them walk all over me. This all changed when I invited a general education teacher to my meeting, and this teacher treated the parents like they were royalty coming to her home and not parents coming to her classroom. She right away told them how she admired them for doing such an excellent job with their son. She thanked them for taking the time to be part of his education, and she treated these parents with the utmost respect. Their son was no angel, and I had heard other teachers blame the parents for raising him to be spoiled and naughty. Instead of an adversarial meeting, the meeting went smoothly as silk, and the parents were on board with helping their son out at home and being available for the school if need be.

After the parents had left, I asked her how she could be so accommodating to them, and she told me that whenever she met parents, she imagined that they were doing the best they knew how with what they had to work with. She reminded me that no one ever receives parent classes in school and that we all learn to be parents from the one model we have, and that is our own parents. I knew my own parents were not perfect, and I knew that my student's parents were probably not perfect either. I saw that although it is challenging to work with children with special needs, at the end of the day, we sent them home, and the parents became responsible. We worked with them one year, three at the most, but their parents had to be responsible for them for the rest of their lives. I suddenly had a newfound respect for parents. I no longer feared them because I now had the tools to make them my partners and not my adversaries. I know that as a parent of a child who had a reading disability, many of my daughter's teachers probably looked at me with blame and judgment, and I fought back with my parental rights. The person who lost this battle was my daughter. Had we had all been partners, there is no telling what we could have accomplished with her.

A facet crucial to partnership is the ability to want the other to succeed more than we ourselves want to succeed. We live in such a competitive world. We go throughout our days comparing ourselves to others and wanting people to fail so that we look better. This has been present everywhere I have looked. In a great partnership, both people are cheering each other on and celebrating each other's successes.

Created Partnership with Difficult People

You might be thinking, "Why would I want to create a partnership with someone that I don't like?" This has been probably true your whole life: when you have trouble with someone, you begin to avoid this person and don't actually try to relate to him or her. You might have many different reasons why a partnership with this person wouldn't work. You might feel that you don't need to get along with this person because he or she affects your life very little. What you don't see is that for every person you push away and avoid, you kill off some of the joy that you could be having in your life. You might think that avoiding that one person in your workplace will not make a difference. Unfortunately, every time you feel that way, you lose some passion for your job, and your job becomes more of a burden to you. You might think that the aunt that you don't care for doesn't affect your life much because you see her only at holiday events. You don't see that this one person can make the holiday events less enjoyable and also affect your interactions with the people you do enjoy. You might think that you will always detest your ex-spouse, so why try? However, you end up affecting the joy that your children have in life as they try to tiptoe around the two of you, trying not to upset either one of you. They become unable to genuinely talk about what is on their minds.

Take time to look at the relationships you have in which you don't like someone and have given up. Look to see what it costs you in your life to continue to be upset with those people.

What is it costing the people around you that are not experiencing the truly loving and joyful you? Ask yourself, "What benefits could I possibly have if I let all my animosity go?" Once you do this and decide that it's time to make some changes in those relationships and create partnerships that were not existent before, you will need to absolutely make a commitment that no matter what it takes, you are going to make it work with these people.

When I decided to take on a partnership with my ex-husband to raise our daughters as equal parents, I knew that it was not going to be an easy task. We had had about ten years of nasty fights, including custody battles and turning each other into Social Services. I saw that my girls were actually suffering having to hear the two of us fight around them. They were becoming manipulative with the two of us and pitting us against each other. My oldest was becoming more and more difficult, and I felt like I could no longer, in reality, do it on my own. I felt that if I could develop a partnership with my ex, we could provide a united front with structures in place to handle our daughters.

After deciding that I wanted this partnership, I had to tell him and to admit the ways that I had been destroying his ability to be that parent to my children. I used to sweep them away from him whenever he had problems with them, and I used to keep him in the dark about what was happening in his children's lives. I had demanded that I have full custody of my girls at my divorce, and I didn't let him have any say about anything. I had felt that I was justified because I felt he didn't make great decisions, he wasn't paying child support, and he had a hot temper. Regardless of my reasons, not having a partner to parent my girls was costing me, and I had to make an effort to stop all my negative behaviors. I let him know that from here on out, I was going to include him in the decisions that affected the girls. I promised that I would leave them with him no matter how hard they cried for me to come get them. I made the commitment that I was no longer going to fight with him because it wasn't beneficial to our partnership. He was shocked that I wanted to make these changes and agreed to do his part in not fighting with me. This wasn't easy at first because we had deep-seated patterns of picking at each other's wounds. I began to say every time I felt attacked that I didn't believe these arguments were beneficial to our partnership. After I had said this, he would drop whatever he was trying to argue with me about, and soon he no longer tried arguing with me.

The next step in creating partnerships with people that you find difficult is to begin to accept them for who they are and for who they aren't. You need to reframe your thoughts about them and start to look for the positives in them. When you notice what they are doing right and reward them for this in some way, then you begin to achieve the partnerships that you desire.

With my ex-husband, I had to acknowledge that he had continued to be in the girls' lives, despite the animosity that we had for each other. That took commitment, and I let him know that I saw this. I acknowledged how hard he worked to make a living. He showed the girls what it meant to work for what you have in life. When he was trying to actually communicate with me instead of fighting, I acknowledged this as well. We soon had a partnership that worked, and I no longer avoided him. To this day, I will go out of my way to make sure that he has a positive relationship with my daughters and grandson. I will sometimes drive him and my daughters somewhere to spend time together.

I used to think that he was the wrong father for my daughters and regretted having children with him. I hated how he treated me and felt like he was an unacceptable father. I hated how he had fathered so many children with different women. I was not that fertile. It took three years to become pregnant the first time and two and a half years after that to get pregnant with my second one. I found out that I have a tilted uterus. Without him, I might not have ever experienced motherhood, and I certainly wouldn't have had the two beautiful daughters that I have now. I see that he was the perfect father that created my daughters to be who they are today. I am proud of them, and I needed him as their father.

Journal activity: Who are some people that you have been avoiding and have written off as people you don't need to spend time on? What does it cost you to avoid them? What is it costing the people you love if you cannot be at least civil to those difficult people, if not working in partnership with them?

Created Dating

So if you have worked on yourself and you feel confident and happy alone and would like to see what kind of relationship you can attract, this is the right chapter for you. If you feel like you desperately need someone in your life, or you recently got out of a long-term relationship and are feeling lonely and vulnerable, you are probably not ready for this. Continue to create you as a self and come back later.

What Do You Want?

You might be thinking that you don't know what you want, but you will know it when you see it. You are not creating your relationship, but wasting a lot of time in the wrong relationships. Not that wrong relationships are bad. We sometimes need them so that we can hone in on what we do want. To spend relationship after relationship with the same kind of person that doesn't work is wasting your time. So stop letting the wrong relationships come your way and begin creating what you want.

In fact, you might have a relationship from your past where you intensely loved a person, but the relationship still failed. It failed because love is sometimes not enough; you have to have that right person. This individual from the past clearly was not the right person for you. You might be continually looking for this same kind of person so that you can fix these mistakes and force it to work this time. It's time to stop this pattern now because it won't work. You've already seen that your past partner was the wrong person to make it work.

We all have a type that we are attracted to, and most of the time, it has to do with physical appearance and not much else. Relationships that are solely based on appearance are short-lived and not fulfilling. There are plenty of models out there that complain that their dates usually lose interest in them after a while. If the only virtue they put forth on their dates is their looks, people do lose interest because there is not enough to sustain a longer relationship.

You might have some criteria like "the other person must have a job and a car and not have a criminal record" and haven't gone beyond that. You might have an extensive list that goes on and on. Whatever vision you might have about the partner you want hasn't worked so far if you are reading this chapter. You need to be looking at how you want to feel in a relationship, what your values are that you want to stand true to, and what kind of activities would you love to share with that person.

What Do You Want to Feel?

This might seem like a stupid question, and you want to answer it with, "I want to feel happy" or "I want to feel loved." Feeling happy and loved is short-lived, and these feelings don't always get to the heart of what you actually want to feel. To answer this question, you need to look at the good and the bad moments of past relationships. When did you feel your best, like you were on top of the world, and when did you feel horrible, like you wanted to crawl into a hole and not have another relationship again? Look at the dreadful moments and ask yourself what you wanted to feel in those moments. Did you want to feel trusted, but were constantly questioned? Did you want to feel safe, but felt you had to watch what you said because it might cause that person to become abusive to you? Did you want to feel accepted, but felt that whatever you said was going to be criticized? Did you want to feel heard?

In my first marriage, I settled pretty quickly on the first guy I thought I loved. He wasn't attentive; however, I didn't know that I needed that. One night at a party, two months after I had married my husband, I found myself talking to a man who had needed some air, just as I had. When I spoke, he listened to me as if I was fascinating, and he asked questions, and this made me feel heard. This was what I had needed and didn't know I needed.

In that same marriage, I noticed that my husband put me down a lot and made me feel small and insignificant. I need relationships now where I'm supported, and the person believes in me and what I can do. I want relationships where I am valued and respected. It's sometimes our most horrendous relationships that teach us what we don't want and open the doors for what we do want.

You might have had some valuable moments in your past, and you want to experience moments like that again. Maybe you had a person who opened doors for you, and this made you feel appreciated. Maybe this person complimented you, and it made you feel beautiful or handsome. Maybe this person did tasks for you out of the blue, and this is what made you feel valuable. Whatever it was, you need to take notice of this because you will then see when you are feeling this way in a relationship. This doesn't need to fit what other people think is what works either.

I knew a woman who had been married to a man for twenty years, and the people around her felt sorry for her because they felt like her husband controlled her. When you asked her what she saw in him, she would say that she liked that her husband took charge in many situations. She had been a single mother for quite a while and didn't want to have to make the decisions for their marriage. She wanted to feel secure, and he provided this for her. It didn't matter what other people thought; she was happy.

Journal activity: What is it that you want to feel in your relationships? What have you learned was missing from past relationships that you want to have in your relationships going forward?

Values

The old saying that opposites attract is merely an old saying. You need to look at your values and decide what you most value in yourself and others. If you value saving money, you don't want to marry someone who throws money away left and right. If you value others' feelings, you don't want to marry someone who treats others like they are beneath him or her. This person will eventually treat you that way as well, and you don't want that. If you have spiritual beliefs that are important to you, you ought to look for someone who has those same beliefs and attends the same services. It is important to discover whether you value having children or not and whether it is a deal breaker if the other person wants or does not want to have children. Your philosophies on raising children are important to compare as well.

Journal activity: Go back to the chapter on commitment and look at the values you listed as important to you. Then list the values that your mate must have.

Activities

Couples don't have to spend every waking minute together doing the same activities, although it is nice to share some of the same interests. If you have some hobbies that you spend a lot of time with, you need to look for someone that likes those hobbies as well, or you won't be spending much time together.

I know a man who loves to play music and be a part of a band. He is actually exceptional at it too. He can play different instruments and is an amazing singer as well. He married a woman who hated the club scene and hated the attention that he got when he was playing in front of others, especially the attention from women. To save his marriage, he had to give up this passion and would restrict himself to jamming with friends in his own house. He values his marriage and family and is willing to do this. If he had created a relationship that was conducive to his musical passions, he might still be playing in public.

Sometimes our hobbies are solely enjoyable little activities that are nice to share with someone. Although it's not what we would call a deal breaker if the person is not interested in it, it can be fun all the same. I once had a boyfriend who liked to do crossword puzzles together. I wasn't into crossword puzzles at the time. I found that as I got better, it was an entertaining activity to share. I took this into my next relationship, and luckily, he liked it as well.

Maybe you like to travel and would like someone to see the sights with you. Maybe you like adventuring with friends and would love someone that supported this and stayed home to watch the house. You don't want your partner spending every moment with you because you need your independence as well, and it is healthy to have separate interests.

I used to like the club scene and dancing. I had a boyfriend who didn't like dancing, although he didn't mind if I had an enjoyable time on the dance floor. He would step away from me on purpose so that someone would ask me to dance. I would then catch a glimpse of him from time to time watching me and smiling because he knew that at the end of the night, I was going to go home with him.

Journal activity: What are some activities that you spend a lot of your time doing and would love someone to share these activities with? What are some activities that you would not mind doing alone or with your friends and would want someone to support you doing these activities?

Created Date

Now that you have an idea of what you want in a romantic relationship, it is time to look for it and take action. Thought with no action is only a thought. Only in the fairy tales does the prince seek you out and sweep you off your feet. In real life, your soulmate doesn't know who you are if you hide at home.

Where to Look

You might be wondering where to look and the best place to look. You should be looking in places where you are spending hours of your time. Begin to tell people around you what you are looking for, and ask if they know of anyone that might fit the profile of what you want. Let them know that you are open to new experiences. Get out there and find places to go to where there might be singles. All those events that come your way on Facebook are an invitation to go meet people. The more people you meet, the better your chances are of finding the person you are creating. Take classes in hobbies that you are interested in, and there might be single people taking those same classes.

In today's computer age, we can go online and literally shop for relationships. You can put up your profile and advertise for what you are looking for. Now that you have done a lot of work on yourself, and you know who you are, it is time to write a fitting profile that sells you. Even if you don't want to do internet dating, writing a profile is excellent practice for when someone asks you about yourself. You will have plenty of positive aspects in mind, and you will be able to state what you are looking for as well.

Many dating sites cater to your interests, and some have compatibility tests that match you up. You can also find sites that will match you to someone that shares your faith. I tried several dating sites and found them to be a lot of fun. Not only could I look around at others' profiles, but I could also write a description that indeed fit me and what I was looking for. This was better than meeting men in a bar because I could look to see whether they had children or wanted children, what kind of jobs they had, and what they wrote about themselves to see if they were a match to what I was looking for. It wasn't ideal, and I had to actually go out on dates to get to know people better; however, it was an excellent start.

Journal activity: Sit and write a shining profile of who you are, your interests, and what you are looking for in a partner. Make sure it is honest and reflects exactly who you are.

Created Courage in Dating

I have seen many people who seem outgoing and bold, but when it comes to them actually asking for a number or giving someone their number, they freeze up. It's that dreadful rejection that they fear. They want desperately to find a person that they can connect with; however, the thought of actually putting themselves out there is too powerful to overcome the need for companionship.

This affects men and women alike. I coached a man who was heading up and running his own company and taking risks every day in his business. We were doing an exercise together where I needed to say no to him. He had to pick a scenario where he hated hearing the word no. He picked asking a person on a date as his scenario. He tried asking me several times, and whenever I said no, I could see the pain in his face. He was personable, sincere, and confident. If I hadn't already been living with someone, I would have dated him in a heartbeat. I knew there were many women out there that would have loved to date him as well, but they wouldn't have the chance as long as he was hung up on not being able to ask them out.

I luckily got through this fear at a young age. I used to go skating when I was around the age of thirteen. When a couples' skate would start, I would stand on the sidelines with the lights dimming and wish that I had someone to hold hands with and skate. I told my brother this, and he took off without my permission to find someone to skate with me. I was surprised when someone took him up on this and skated up to me and asked me to skate. From then on out, I would pick a person I wanted to skate with and send my brother over there. My brother became interested in girls as well and would sometimes ask a girl to skate, so I was left without my matchmaker. I finally gathered up my own courage and began asking boys to skate. Some said no; however, many of them said yes.

I learned to read a boy's body language and know whether I had a chance with him. If he looked my way or smiled, I knew I had a shot. I made it a game to smile back and flirt with them, and at times, they came over and asked me before I could ask them. I gained confidence in the dating world, and I took that into my adult years when I wanted to dance with someone. It only took practice, and that is my advice to you if you want to ask someone out or to give your number away. Hold your head high and do it. There are probably many people who would love to go out with you that are only waiting for you to ask or to give some indication that you are available.

If you are terrified of that rejection, find a person that you feel safe with and ask them to play the part of someone you want to date. Have them tell you "No," "I'm not interested," "Not with you," or any other line that you are afraid of hearing and practice being gracious to the other person for taking the time to hear you out. You will begin to grow in your confidence from simply practicing.

Homework activity: Go out and ask as many people as you can for a date. Don't be attached to what they say. If you hear a lot of no answers, seek out a trusted friend and practice. Ask what you might be doing wrong. This person will probably see some way that you are inauthentic instead of confident.

Challenging Your Beliefs

Many people go into dates with a negative attitude toward males or females. They might think that men are always after sex or that women only want to use them for their money. When you have ideas like this already in your head, it can be hard to have a relaxing date because you are on your guard the whole time. The other person might also sense this distrust and guardedness and feel you don't like him or her. You will be looking for evidence to prove what you think is right instead of noticing your date's positive aspects.

I did this when I first became single after my divorce. I had hung out in bars where there was a lot of drinking going on, and many men I met were looking to find someone to go home with at the end of the night. I began thinking that men only wanted sex from me and would try to pressure me into it if they had any indication that I was that kind of woman. I would spend my entire dates trying to keep my distance and not present myself as too available. I'm sure I was unpleasant to go out with, and that is why I got a lot of first dates but never second ones. Later on, when I learned to let go of my negative predispositions about men, I began to let my hair down on first dates and let a man see me for who I authentically was. I began to have men ask me out on second and third dates and so on.

We need to work through and challenge these beliefs that we have toward the sex that we are dating. We need to get in touch with the reasons that we love them, such as "I love having a strong male presence wrap his arms around me" or "I love how a woman smiles at me when I've said something somewhat clever." When you get in touch with how fond you are of the entire gender before going out on a date, you create an acceptance for whoever the other person is, and that is appealing to your date.

There are plenty of reasons why you are attracted to this gender and not another gender, and many of them could be pretty juicy. Let yourself fantasize about those reasons, and let yourself fall in love with either men or women all over again. Let yourself believe that yes, some of them fit your negative predispositions, but not all them are that way.

As you have preconceived notions about the opposite gender, you might also have stereotypes about your own sex and how you should or shouldn't behave on a date. You might think that men should always pay or that women should always wear sexy outfits or that women should always wear a blouse that is not too revealing. When you believe stereotypes about your own gender, you are putting yourself in a box that maybe you don't fit. You are not allowing yourself to be authentic as the real person you are.

You might carry some negative baggage around about what love, romance, and dating are. You might believe that romance is not real or is expensive. You might believe some of the old songs that say that love hurts. You might hate dating and want to settle down as soon as possible. All these notions are playing in the background, directing what you say and do on a date. This does not reflect the positive person you are. For example, if you think that romance is expensive, you might spend a lot of money that you don't have on a date and put forth an image that you are not going to be able to sustain in the long run. If you think that love is painful, you might not let yourself be vulnerable and open up to another human being.

To challenge these false assumptions, you need to ask yourself if these notions are always true or whether you suddenly made them up after a bad date or relationship. You need to look at the influence that these negative assumptions are having on your relationships. You need to actually turn these assumptions into positives and begin telling yourself positive messages instead.

Journal activity: Finish the following sentences. Men are always _____. Women are always _____. Love is _____. Romance is _____. Dating is _____. If you find that you have negative views when you finish these sentences, begin putting positive words and phrases in these sentences that contradict what you think.

Creating Dates Ahead of Time

You worked through what you would like to feel in a relationship, and you can start feeling that before you go out on a date. If you want to feel valued, then adore yourself and expect that the other person will pick up on your sense of self and value you as well. If you want to feel trusted, then imagine the other person trusting you and opening up to you. Imagine the other person feeling comfortable enough to be authentic in your presence. Take time to passionately create how you want your date to go. Imagine yourself having fun, flirting, being comfortable, and allowing yourself to be authentic. This will set you up to actually make this happen on the date.

Before going out on a first date, it is beneficial to think about your characteristics that make you *you*. It is important that you let the real you shine on a date so that the other person has an excellent first impression of you. This might take you some time looking at your characteristics and deciding which positive aspects of yourself would you like to put forward for others to see. Imagine yourself out on your date, actually showing those positive aspects of yourself. You want to be someone that your date will remember and not forget the minute he or she gets back in the car to go home. Maybe you have some compelling stories about yourself that are funny, but not too intimate, that you like to share. You have to be interested in yourself and your own life to have others see you as stimulating.

One of the idiosyncrasies that people find fascinating about me is that I used to be a security guard in hospitals. I not only helped tie down patients; I also had to escort dead bodies to the morgue. I have story after story about my life as a security guard, and I have found that people are surprised that I did this and become unusually absorbed in the stories as well. It intrigues people and makes them interested in getting to know me better because they want to know how a person like me can be loving, yet take a job where I have to be the tough guy.

As you would like to share curious facts on a first date, there are intimacies you should not share right away with a stranger. There are personal secrets that could actually scare a new person away. These people have not earned the right to hear these stories as of yet, and they need to be reserved till a time when you want to begin to develop intimacy.

Journal activity: Make a list of some of the stories that make you seem compelling. Rank these stories as ones that you could share on a first date, ones to tell on a second date, and some that you will reserve for when you are intimate and trusting toward someone.

Making a Positive Impression

So you finally attain that first date, and you are wondering what to say or do to make a positive impression. You might be thinking questions like "What if they don't like me?" This mindset does not set you up for what you created for this date. All you need to be thinking is that you are out to make a new friend today. If you were going to have coffee or lunch with a new coworker, would you be worried about whether that person might be the one you wanted to spend your life with? No! You would be trying to get to know the person better so that you can be friendly with him or her in the office. This is how a date should be: a chance to get to know a person, and for that person to get to know you. You wouldn't bare your soul to a new coworker because the coworker hasn't earned that right or that trust yet, and you shouldn't bare your soul to the stranger you have a first date with either. You wouldn't be judging and weighing all a coworker says to you, evaluating whether this is the right person to have children with, and you shouldn't be doing this on a first date either. Many times, people are nervous on first dates, and your sole purpose should be to put your date at ease so he or she can behave more authentically. Looking past the masks that many people put on for a first date can be helpful in seeing whether this person fits what you want.

During my separation from my husband, I met a sexy male dancer at a bar. He was gorgeous, and when he asked for my number, I was shocked that he wanted to spend time with me over the other beautiful ladies in the bar. I felt that my husband had rejected me, and I wanted the attention of a gorgeous Adonis. He called me and asked if he could come over to my house. I was hesitant and lousy about my boundaries at that time. I let him come over. He came over expecting that I wanted to have sex with him. We talked instead. Mostly, he talked, and I provided the comfortable place to listen. I found out a lot about him and his life. I learned that he had a girlfriend that he was living with. They were having problems. I discovered, as handsome as I thought he was, he struggled with self-esteem. I listened to him, and he began to feel a sense of his own worth. When he left, he was going home to his girlfriend to make up. I highly doubt this fixed his self-esteem, and he probably sought out the attention of other girls to find it; however, I learned that handsome men are not always what they seem.

Being Attentive

Just as I was attentive with my male dancer friend, it is important to be present and attentive on a date. Not only for the other person's sake, but for your own sake. You should look your date in the eye as he or she talks and lean in to hear what he or she has to say. People love others that are attentive to them. Dale Carnegie's book *How to Win Friends and Influence People* was all about this. It helps to have a genuine interest in others and what they want to convey. As you listen and show acceptance of other people, they begin to get comfortable and accept you.

I remember being somewhat standoffish during my dates because I didn't want to lead anyone on until I knew whether I liked him or not. I know now that I probably missed some outstanding chances to make some profound connections with some genuine people because I was not letting them be themselves with me. It was not loving of me, and that was the reason I was not finding the love that I wanted. If you want to have love in your life, it is important to be loving first. Who knows? Even if the person in front of you is not your soulmate, being attentive could help you decide this. You might discover that this person is a better match for someone you know. Or this person might know someone who is ideal for you.

Being attentive is being present to what is happening. Notice what this person says and how he or she treats you and others, and especially, be present with how you are feeling on the date. Being present allows you to stay in the moment and not let old habits, fears, or conversations come into play that can take you out of the moment. Notice when you are not authentic and try to bring yourself back to who you know yourself to be. If being your authentic self on a date is all you have achieved, then you have at least gained a victory over your past, when you have had to be somebody else to impress someone else. Let yourself get to know this person as if you were making a new friend, and be open to having a second date with this person. Most people are not authentic on their first dates and don't open up to their true selves until the second or third date. You might find a very charming person on the next date that you would have never seen because they were too nervous on the first date.

As I say, be open to a second date. I'm not saying that you must go on a second date with this person. If you find that this person is not whole and seems to be broken, or there is a creepy vibe about the individual, hold your boundaries and do not let it go beyond this date. If you are someone who in the past has taken on people as projects and tried to fix them, then make sure you are not going out with people who are looking for others to fill in their gaps and complete them. You have worked too hard on yourself to be that person. You are a healthy person seeking another healthy person that you can have a healthy relationship with.

Created Boundaries

When we are dating, and the other person is giving to us, we might feel that we are obligated to give back. This might make us uncomfortable because the relationship is new and we might not know what the other person is expecting in return. We might need to take some space at times or accept that others need space as well and that space is healthy in a relationship. People who have too many expectations in their relationships and don't give others space to breathe, create co-dependency. This is not healthy.

When you are going out on dates, it is fine to allow a person to contribute what he or she wants to provide to you, and to not feel obliged to reciprocate. This is true for women in relationships. They might not want a man to buy dinner because they will feel that they will have to somehow repay him with physical favors. This does not allow the man to contribute to her and help her to feel special. This ties his hands. Now, not all men pay for dates; however, not allowing him to pay when he apparently wants to pay can say to a man that you don't need him. When a man does pay for the dinner, it is not expected that she has to reciprocate in any way. Anyone that makes her feel like she is now obliged to give what she is not comfortable in giving, such as hugs, kisses, or sex, is not ready for a healthy relationship.

This goes for a man as well. He does not have to take a woman to expensive places because a woman is beautiful and is willing to go out with him. He should not give more to the relationship than he is comfortable giving. If a woman expects you to spend a lot of money on her and you cannot sustain this over an extended period of time, it is probably better to stop seeing her than to present yourself as someone you are not. This will cause heartache and pain for all in the long run.

When you are developing a relationship with anyone, you should see your company as enough for anyone. If you are giving of yourself through your attention, your appreciation, your listening, and your presence to what the other person needs, you are giving enough to the relationship and should not have to work at being loved by the other. You are either loved for being who you are or not.

This goes for your attitude as well when dating. You should rarely expect your partner to have to prove his or her love for you. You don't want the other person to have to change who he or she is to accommodate you because that is not letting the other person be authentic. Your partner might be willing to accommodate you in the beginning when the chemistry of falling in love is present, although most will not sustain this forever. Having a person's love should be enough for you because you already have the love you need, and that is inside yourself. You don't need to test others to see if they love you. To feel love, all you need to do is to give love without the expectation of it coming back. If it does come back to you, that is great. If it does not come back to you, that is great as well because it was you giving the gift of unconditional love that allowed you the experience of love, not the other person reciprocating in some way.

Confronting Your Preconceptions

We harbor and carry so many preconceptions about dating rituals. We have beliefs about a kiss, we have biases about too many calls or not enough calls, we have preconceptions about sex, and we have presumptions about meeting someone's family. We have tremendous preconceptions about saying "I love you" to a person. The damaging part about these misconceptions is that we expect others to have the same preconceptions about these dating rituals as us, and when they don't, there is miscommunication. It is important to see the other person's point of view around their beliefs so that the two of you can be on the same page when it comes to these so-called benchmarks in a relationship.

I was in a three-year relationship with a man, and although I had told him several times that I loved him, he had never said it back to me. This made me feel that I was wasting my time in the relationship and giving more of myself than he was. I felt like I couldn't express my love to him openly because it seemed to make him uncomfortable hearing it. I didn't like the feeling of not being fully self-expressed in this relationship. Instead of dumping him, I waited until one night when the two of us were close and being open with each other and brought up the subject of love.

"Why don't you tell me you love me?" I asked in an open and understanding way and not in an accusatory fashion. I knew that if I came at him in a confronting way, I would probably not discover what he had to say, and I would possibly push him away.

He answered, " I don't say that I love you because I really don't know that I want to marry you and settle down with you."

Light bulbs went off inside my head. I realized that he thought to say he loved someone committed himself to marriage, family and a shared house. I was relieved to hear this because I was not sure that he was the man I wanted to marry either. I saw that when I said I loved him, he must have thought that I was trying to push him into a marriage.

"I'm not sure I want to get married either, but I still know that I love you," I responded, and could see the relief on his face. "Do you think about me when you are away from me?" I asked deciding to see if he loved me by my definition.

"Yes"

"Do you care about my well-being and want me to be happy?"

"Yes"

"Do you feel close to me and happy when you are around me?"

"Yes"

"Then by my definition of love, you love me."

"Then by your definition, I love you, " he said finally. I had waited years to hear this, and this was a great relief, although I knew in my heart that he did. After this, he was freer to say that he loved me, and I was more open to say that I loved him. We had developed a shared definition of love that we could agree upon.

What I learned from this experience was that I needed to not only explain myself but to ask questions as well. I naturally love people, and I'm willing to tell people that I love them. I let them know my definition of love in the process. I let them know that to me, love means that I accept them for who they are and who they are not. I let them know that I have no expectations of them to earn my love. When someone says he or she loves me, I ask what this means to that person so that I have a clear understanding of the other person's feelings and expectations for the relationship. I do not want someone to think that when I say "I love you," it really means "I want to marry you."

Taking Space

There will be times when you are dating when you get caught up in the whole experience, and you feel you are losing your perspective. You might not be taking care of some of your priorities or your health., You may feel that you need to take a step back and collect your thoughts. You might not be the one that takes the space; maybe the other person needs the space. This is all natural in dating and is healthy, except that sometimes our fear of abandonment will kick in, and we will have a sense that the relationship is falling apart.

It is important to actually slow the relationship down at times and breathe. If you don't, you might find yourself in way over your head and possibly married without first evaluating whether this is the right relationship for you. The hormones produced in the first three months can be intensely powerful. They might be delicious and exhilarating, but not necessarily how you want to live your whole life. So whether you take the space, or your newfound date takes the space, it can give you perspective and can be beneficial for the relationship, not necessarily bad.

If you are taking the space, realize that this could activate some fears in the other person. Your date might see it as a rejection or think that you want to see other people, and not understand the benefit to him or her. Your date might invade your space or need reassurances that you are not ending the relationship. Being patient with the other person can be trying. You have to realize that you have probably been in those shoes as well. Give the other person promises of when you will call or get together, and keep your promises.

If you are the one that the other person is taking a break from, tell yourself that this is for the better, not the worse. Begin thinking about the tasks you can accomplish during the time that you are apart. Set up a time to see people that you have been neglecting during your whirlwind romance. Avoid the constant texting or calling to see what the other person is doing with his or her time. This comes off as needy and can drive the other person further away from you. Assure yourself that the space you are letting your date take will allow him or her the chance to miss you and might create a closer bond with this person.

During the space that you take away from the person you are dating, take the time to step back and look to see whether this person is what you created as a future partner. Does this person have the values that you were looking for? Does this person treat you the way you wanted to be treated? Is this a person that you think could be a real partner in life and support your goals as well? Sometimes when you see a person every day, and you are having those chemical reactions to the other person's presence, you are not actually taking a look at the big picture. Make sure to slow the affair down once in a while to sincerely consider this.

Getting Physical

There are many opinions on when to become physical with a newfound interest, and this can be entirely up to you and what is comfortable for you. I know that I tended to get physical in my dating relationships too early, and although I felt like I could handle the fallout, I rarely took into consideration the people that I was becoming physical with and how they were becoming attached to me. Having sex in relationships can sometimes create meanings in your or someone else's mind. You might think that if you have sex with someone too soon, the other person will think you are too easy and take advantage of you. If you wait too long, the other person might believe that you don't want to have sex with him or her. If you have sex with him or her, then the other person might feel that you are now taking the relationship to the next level, or that you love him or her. There are so many meanings that we give sex in dating relationships that it is hard to have perspective about the relationship.

I have to say that you know yourself best. If you can be careful about it and keep your feelings in check as well as communicate openly what this does and doesn't mean for the relationship, then go ahead and allow yourself that pleasure when you want it. If you know that the minute you have sex with a new partner, you are going to lose respect for yourself or your partner, then wait until you feel that it is more appropriate and can mean more to you.

You might want to wait till you are in an exclusive relationship with this person. You don't want to find out later down the line that you had given up seeing other people when you began sleeping with someone, and the person you are sleeping with doesn't see it this way. Once again, clear communication is the key here. Never assume that the other person is on the same page as you without receiving clarification.

Journal activity: Look at how soon you become physical with a person in a relationship. How has it affected your perspectives on those relationships? Do you think the people whom you got physical with might have been hurt in the process? What do you see yourself doing differently in future relationships?

Created Breakups

Although this book is based on creating relationships, it is inevitable that breakups are going to happen, that people are going to have to let others go, and that there are going to be people that leave you. What hurts about this whole scenario is what we say to ourselves when this happens. If you are the one that decides to end the relationship, you may feel like you failed. When the breakup happens to you, you may come away with the feeling that you are broken, and it doesn't necessarily have to be that way. If you are creating your relationships, you can look at the breakup like Edison looked at a failed attempt at a light bulb. You have one more person you have tried and have experienced one more person that doesn't work for you. You can use this insight going into other relationships until you finally make it right. Edison didn't give up on the light bulb, and you don't need to give up on relationships.

Non-Created Breakups

Most of us have had at least one non-created breakup, if not many. When you have not thought about the best way of parting with someone, you might leave the other person with unanswered questions and struggling to move on toward new relationships. You might have had a hasty breakup, where it was done in the heat of the moment, and you didn't have the facts straight. You might have played superficial games to make the breakup seem mutual. You might have recently abandoned someone with no forwarding address or sent an e-mail to say goodbye. All these types of breakups are more painful and leave people with many unanswered questions. In the world of being loving people, we do not want to leave others with such pain.

You might be thinking about some of the breakups you have had in the past and regretting them. Having broken up with many men, I have a few regrets myself regarding my methods, and thus this chapter has been a difficult one to write. When I wanted out of a relationship, I would begin distancing myself, asking for space and time away from my partner, which was in reality time to go out with someone else and see if I liked him better. This usually happened around three months into a relationship because that was when the lustful chemicals started wearing off in my system and I would want more.

I once was living with a man and, after a fight, took off and went looking at houses. I found one I liked and put in a bid on it on that same day. I was already out the door before the fight. I wasn't honest about it. I unfortunately drew this relationship out further because I didn't break up with him when I left. I was not adept at breaking hearts and would let relationships go on far longer than I wanted. The communication was not there, and instead, I would play sneaky games.

Decision to Break Up

The decision to break up can be a hard one. What you need to do is to look at whether the person you are in a relationship with, whether it be a friend or a lover, treats you with respect. Do you feel that this person is in your corner and is willing to pick you up and push you forward? If you said yes, then you have a hard decision to make. If you said no, then this is probably a person that you need to let go. You need to ask yourself whether this person is giving or is most often taking from you. There should be give and take in all relationships. If this person is mainly a negative drain on you, then you should probably let him or her go. Some acceptable reasons to break up a relationship are catching the other person in betrayal or noticing that the other person lies to you a lot. Or this person doesn't have any consideration for you, breaks a lot of dates, or shows up late most of the time. This person is abusive in some way, either to you or to other people. This person is extremely jealous of the time you spend with others or of what you are doing and becoming in your life. Your best thermometer about whether the relationship works for you is how you feel when you are with that person. If you leave mad, upset, degraded, or hurt after seeing that person, it's probably time to get out and not waste any more time in a relationship that is not nurturing to you.

Sometimes you feel unsure of what is wrong with a relationship, and you need to figure out what is happening. You want to know whether it is on the other person's part or yours. This can be where you step outside yourself, pretend to be a friend to you, and give yourself advice coming from a neutral place. If you have trouble stepping outside yourself, talk to your friends; however, make sure they are neutral friends and not ones that you have turned against this person.

It is always best to go directly to the other person you are thinking of breaking up with and talking with him or her about these thoughts. This way the other person might not feel blind-sided by a breakup. Many of us feel helpless to fix a relationship that doesn't feel right, although talking to the person can help quite a bit.

I had one man who was receptive to talking about our relationship, and we had many discussions about what was going on. He would tell me that he wasn't satisfied with my passion or reactions to his gifts, and I would talk about how I sadly wanted to love him but didn't feel in love with him. We felt that we should love each other because we had many interests in common. Unfortunately, we could also see that it wasn't satisfying for either one of us. We ended up breaking up amicably and stayed friends for many years after our breakup because we had been so open with our communication and hadn't burned our bridges. He remained in touch with my children, which was important to them.

If you are ready to talk to the person, here are a few tips.

- You need to speak in "I" statements that are not accusatory. This will allow the other person to listen and not put him or her on the defensive.
- Let the person know ahead of time what you want to talk about and when, so you can both can be prepared.

- Acutely listen to the other person and encourage the other person to open up so that you can hear what he or she is saying.
- Let the other person know that you are not breaking up now. Tell your partner that you are having thoughts about the subject and would like to discuss them.
- Suggest trying new ideas that you have never tried, such as a vacation, coaching, a retreat, or therapy. Becoming unstuck from a boring relationship can be trying a new approach to relating.

Non-Romantic Breakup

So if you have decided that the best course you have with this person is to break up, it is best to create a plan for this. If it is a non-romantic person that you can spend less time with, then it might not be as difficult. It's always best to talk to the other person and explain that you won't be doing any more activities with him or her, and why. This way, the other person is not trying to make plans with you becoming more and more angry that you are not spending time with him or her. This could be a time for the other person to learn a lesson about him- or herself and what it might be costing him or her to influence others in a negative way. The person might thank you later for letting him or her know. Make sure you are honest with your concerns and make it more about you and the way it feels when you're around this person than it is about him or her. You might have already been distancing yourself from this person, and all that is left is to unfriend them on "Facebook" or deleting their number on your phone.

I know someone that has her own business, and she had a client that was often late to appointments, or would send a payment that would not go through. She finally sat this client down and had a talk with her about how this was affecting her business. She let this woman know that she valued their longstanding relationship, but that this was not working, and that she would need to make her appointments on time and pay with cash or find someone else. The woman agreed to this but was once again late to another appointment. The business owner then decided to cut ties with this woman and was willing to let her know why.

Romantic Breakup

If you are planning on breaking up a serious relationship, that might need more planning. Here are some steps you can follow.

1. Plan the day that works for this breakup. Find people to support you in your plan, and let them know how they can help. Maybe you will need a support person to call or someone to go out with on the days that you are typically seeing your former lover.

2. Set goals for the breakup. Do you want a clean break where it is done and over and neither one of you contact each other or do you want a breakup where you continue to speak to each other on occasion? Are there children involved, and if so, do you want the kids to know that it isn't their fault and to continue to feel secure in knowing that they are not losing either one of their parents? Do you want to leave a betrayed situation with your head held high and not look back? You get to create this. Focus on how you want to feel afterward, not what you are afraid of feeling. Picture yourself in the future, confident about the way the relationship went, and bring that feeling into the present as you think about how you want the breakup to go. If you are married or living together, you ought to begin separating your finances and finding ways that you can support yourself on your own. You might start to seek legal counsel if you foresee a messy breakup.

3. Unless this person is abusive and possessive and you will need to make a quick getaway, start to have discussions about your intentions and what works best for the two of you and the children, if there are any. Talk about whether you want a complete split or merely a separation and what that will look like. Too many people suddenly up and leave,

meaning to have a separation, but don't discuss what they want that separation to look like. They don't consider whether they are going to talk daily or weekly, or whether they will go on dates with each other or other people. With all this left unsaid, it is no wonder that feelings get hurt during separation, and it becomes impossible to repair the damage.

When the two of you are communicating, you get to create what the separation looks like and what you hope to accomplish with the separation. There is no one way that this needs to look either. I knew a couple that got a divorce and remained best friends and lovers for years afterward, except in their own homes. I knew a couple where one person lived on one floor of the home with her new husband, and her ex-husband lived in the basement of the home with his new wife, and they shared the responsibilities of their children amicably. Make sure as you have talks about what comes next that it is fair to both parties.

The Breakup

So now that you have most the details worked out, it is time to take the next step, and that is going through with the breakup. You are not responsible for what your partner will feel, do, or say after the breakup. You are responsible for how you deliver it. There might be some thought of going out with a grand gesture in a relationship where you were betrayed; however, the best revenge is always to come out the other end happy and confident. The other person might go from relationship to relationship, leaving havoc in his or her wake, and sadly, he or she might not experience the real true love that happens after many faithful years together. You, on the other hand, will as long as you can put this experience in your past and leave it there.

We all would desire a peaceful breakup where both parties leave with good grace, and there is no lingering pain or anger, but this rarely happens. There is usually someone who wanted the relationship to be more than it was. In breakups, we need closure. Closure means there is nothing left unsaid and no questions unanswered. The relationship is clearly over, and there are no leftover residual "what ifs" or "maybe I could haves." People need closure in relationships, and a quick e-mail, text, or voicemail is a cop-out and doesn't provide the person with the necessary closure to move on in his or her life. If we remember that all relationships provide lessons for the future, without closure and knowing what truly happened, people are left wondering what they did or didn't do. Be prepared to take responsibility for what you might have done or said that led the other person to believe the relationship was better than it was in actuality. Be prepared to be honest about any indiscretions you might have had. Your partner will sense it and want to know the truth. You might be going against promises you have made to that person about marriage or the future, and you need to take responsibility for that as well.

I one time had a lover break up with me in an e-mail on Valentine's Day. I had truly loved this man, and I foolishly sent him an e-mail saying that I never wanted to talk to him again. This left me without the closure I needed to move on. I spent five years wondering what had happened and why we didn't work out. I finally got back in touch with him when I saw that I couldn't seem to move on in relationships, and I got the closure I needed.

Honesty is important, but be careful not to be cruel. You should say what you need to say carefully and stick to your "I" statements. It's better to say, "I don't feel we are sexually compatible" as opposed to "You are terrible in bed." You should be clear, but caring. By caring, you should give caring and genuine messages to the other person, and avoid pointing fingers at him or her. Make sure to be present and in control, and not let the other person's pain or lashing out take you away from the goals that you wish to accomplish. Don't be drawn into fights or get defensive when the other person says words that hurt you. Acknowledge your partner's pain and anger and show compassion for him or her. Avoid giving messages that will suggest that there is still a chance with you. Being compassionate should not look like you are still in love with the other person. You can leave the door open for more questions and for the other person to tell you what he or she needs to say to you at a later date. Remember the times when you said to yourself that you wished you had said what you felt or asked a question and regretted that you didn't. Getting complete can take more than one conversation sometimes. If the other person asks questions that you do not know the answer to, explain that you had not thought about this and will need time to think about it. It is better to give truthful answers than ones that are made up on the spot. Those answers rarely seem to make sense to the person that you are giving them to.

You should acknowledge the other person for what you have learned from the relationship. Acknowledge the wonderful experiences the person is leaving you with as well as the time and effort that he or she put into the relationship. Give positive messages about what you wish and see for the other person's future. Let the other person know that there are going to be plenty of partners that will genuinely appreciate him or her as well.

Having Your Heart Broken

Inevitably, someone leaves us, and we are left feeling heartbroken. This opens old wounds of sometime in our past when a parent left us, even if it was only for a short while. We have a sense of entitlement that people we love must stay with us and not ever leave. This can happen with friends, family, or lovers. I remember my sadness when my friends from high school began moving to other states to start new lives. I felt that if our bonds of friendship genuinely meant as much to them as to me, they would stay and continue to enjoy the same activities that we did when we were younger. The one real truth in life is that nothing ever remains the same. We are always changing, growing, and moving forward. As we change, so do the people in our lives. They find new interests and passions and have lives of their own, and we don't own them. If we love them, we let them go so that they can continue to grow and love and be loved.

The worst experience that happens when our hearts are broken is that we might end up blaming ourselves during this time and not take care of our mental state. We tell ourselves that we are failures, not good enough in bed, not pretty enough, and many other negative messages that are damaging to our souls. We have thoughts like "I will never trust again" and "I will be alone for the rest of my life." We fear that we will never find someone that we feel that close to again.

It's during this time that we need to start the creation process to prepare ourselves for the next relationship. We need to start with our mindset and think better thoughts, such as "This person was a benefit to me" and "This person was preparing me for a relationship that is going to be far better." This is where you practice forgiveness of yourself and the other person. The other person might have deliberately hurt you during the breakup process; however, many people don't know better ways to end relationships, how to think about the other's feelings during this time, or how to communicate openly about their feelings. We can wish they had, all we want, but forgiveness is letting go of the idea that events could have happened another way. Forgiving a person and letting him or her go without resentment is the best gift you can give that person you loved and yourself. If you do it any other way, you could have regrets for a long time.

My ex-husband and I didn't know how to break up in an amicable way. Our breakup was messy, and it left us both raw and hurt. Although my husband was the one that left and I felt devastated, I had had my own faults in the relationship that I had not been responsible for. For two years after my daughter was born, I hated him. I would write him letters threatening divorce. I didn't support his efforts at trying to get a business going and made him feel bad for not spending enough time with my daughter and me. I despised having sex with him and withheld this whenever I could. I shouldn't have been surprised when he began welcoming attentions from a younger version of me, but I was. He was even honest about his infidelities. I could tell that his indiscretions were causing him guilt, and he would promise to not do them again but would break his word soon after. Instead of letting him go, I tried to manipulate him with sex, which led to more loneliness and pain when he went out the door to her. This was an excruciatingly painful time. I wish I had had the skills then that I have now to deal with these behaviors.

I needed to begin to focus on myself and my baby that I was pregnant with. I got a therapist, who helped me through this and helped me to start to see my life differently. She rarely judged what I said or did and was able to help me to see this whole experience positively. She started me on my path of growth and introduced me to self-help books, which have made an immense difference in my life. It is sometimes the worst times in our lives that make us the strongest and make us proud of who we have become. I wished at that point that I could look into the future, see myself as the strong, independent woman that I am now, and know that the actual events that were destroying me at the time would later make me unstoppable in the world.

You might be at that low point right now reading this book, and I want you to imagine an able you that has gotten through your heartbreak and come out the other side with power and control over your life. What kind of decisions would that person be making in your life right now, and how would that person be handling the breakup? Seeing now what I have become, I can not only forgive my ex-husband but thank him for the lessons he taught me. It's time that we see our relationships as lessons and teachers and not failures in life. The people that have left us left us with new insights and greater clarity as to what does not work for us. We need to wish them well on their journeys so that they can go on to learn their lessons and teach others lessons.

Creating Closure of Past Relationships

So what do you do about past relationships where you don't have closure? What if you are afraid to reach out to the other person because he or she might be married and having a great life and you don't exactly want to hear that? How do you get closure from someone who is suddenly gone with no forwarding address?

Remember my Valentine's Day heartbreak? At least I had numbers for my old boyfriend's sisters. What I didn't have was the courage to call him. I had finally seen what was in the way of having a new boyfriend; however calling him was another matter. I had many thoughts go through my head about whether he was married and happy with his new wife. How would I feel about that, since I had wanted to be the one that he loved and settled down with? I had to look at my real commitment, and that was to find someone special in my life, and five years was enough time to swoon for a man that was no longer there. I had a coach that encouraged me and helped me to move beyond my fear. She was there for me and was not going to let more time in my life go by without getting complete. If you have a chance in your life to have a coach that is committed to you having what you want in your life, you should take it.

I knew that I could take it one step at a time. First, I had to see if my phone numbers still worked and see if his sister would give me his phone number. I knew I could at least make that step. I did and found out he was living with her and was not married. The next step was to call him and reacquaint myself with him. I had to believe that he was willing to help me get complete because we had been friends long before we were lovers. So I finally made the call and took 100 percent responsibility for my e-mail and for saying that I never wanted to hear from him again, when in reality I did and was not complete after the way we broke up. He was glad to hear from me and was willing to talk. We talked about the breakup and the thoughts we had been holding back from each other. After this conversation, the relationship we had was complete. The real kicker to this story is that my growth, honesty, and vulnerability intrigued him, and he wanted to get to know me again. That was ten years ago, and we are still together. That would never have happened if I hadn't called him and moved past the feelings of abandonment and distrust. I would have carried that into all my future relationships and had feared that it would happen again.

I'm not promising that you will be able to get back together with your past lovers, because that might not be in your future, nor should it be your intention. You do have the chance to talk to them and find out what might have happened in those relationships. If you do, and you are scared like I was, have someone in your corner, as I had my coach. Practice what you are going to say to them and how to speak to them so that they are not defensive, and they are willing to open up to you. Write down the questions that you would like answered and tell yourself that no matter what the other person says, you are going to be okay with it. Have your "coach" friend or whoever pretend to be that person you wish to get complete with and answer you with the exact answers you are afraid of hearing. This way, you can practice being okay with it before you have the actual conversation.

In the actual conversation, make sure that you communicate how critical it is to have answers and that without them, you will have unresolved questions. Let the other person know that he or she can be completely honest with you and that you won't attack him or her. Be responsible for the negative influences you had on the relationship and how poorly you might have taken the breakup. Maybe you were the one who broke off the relationship, and you never communicated thoroughly what you needed to. Maybe you were the one that betrayed the other person, and you never sincerely apologized for the betrayal. Whatever was left unsaid at the time of the breakup, here is the chance to get complete. Afterward, thank the other person for helping you get complete and wish the other person well in his or her relationships. Thank the other person for the work that he or she put into the relationship and for how he or she had helped you on your relationship journey. Then say goodbye. Before having this conversation, picture yourself feeling completely free after the goodbye.

Now, some of you might have no clue how to get complete with a past lover. That person might have died, or left without any contact information. The person might have said that he or she never wanted to hear from you again or taken out a restraining order against you. How do you get complete then? This is where you need to use your creating skills. Since you are responsible for your own completion and you can't put the responsibility on someone else to do, act, or feel a way that the person doesn't want to feel, you need to create your own completion.

You can write a letter saying all that you want and need to say to this person and asking the questions that you want to ask. Here's the creative part. You then write a letter back to yourself from that person and include what you would want to hear back in reply to your letter. Include any messages that make you feel complete with the relationship. Let's say that this person cheated on you, and you feel betrayed, and you struggle with trust in your relationships. Write a letter back to yourself with that person

127

regretting what he or she did and apologizing profusely. If you don't have any clue why the person left, make up a story. This story could say that his or her father had died, and he or she now had to move away to take care of his or her aging mother. Make up that the person truly never wanted to interrupt your life. You know best what you would like to hear from that person, so write this back to yourself. Is it the truth? Who knows? More than likely not; however, you can believe it to be the truth if it makes you feel better. Even the truths in life and the reasons that people do what they do don't always make sense.

The next step in this process is to obtain a trusted friend to read you the letter you wrote. It might feel more like it is coming from another person. You can then burn the letter and tell yourself that you forgive the other person for the heartbreak he or she was part of. Forgiveness is the real key to being complete with a relationship. When you forgive another person for not doing, being, or loving you enough, you are then set free to experience love with others.

Bibliography

Chapman, Gary. *The Five Love Languages*. Chicago: Northfield Publishing, 1995.

De Angelis, Barbara. *Are You the One for Me?* New York: Dell Publishing, 1992.

Gray, John PhD. *Mars and Venus in the Bedroom*. New York: Harper Collins Publishers, 1995.

Klein, Marty. *Sexual Intelligence*. New York: Harper Collins Publishers, 2012.

Lerner, Harriet PhD. *The Dance of Anger*. New York: Harper Perennial, 1997.

Lerner, Harriet PhD. *The Dance of Intimacy*. New York: Harper Perennial, 1989.

Peck, M. Scott MD. *The Road Less Traveled*. New York: Simon and Schuster, 1978.

Ruiz, Miguel. *Mastery of Love*. San Rafael, California: Amber-Allen Publishing, 1999.

Vanzant, Iyanla. *In the Meantime*. New York: Simon and Schuster, 1998.

Walsch, Neale Donald. *Conversations with God: An Uncommon Dialogue, Book 3*. Charlottesville, VA: Hampton Roads Publishing Company, Inc., 1998.

Printed in the United States
By Bookmasters